LARA IN AMERICA

LARA
IN AMERICA

Adrianne Cooper

David McKay Company, Inc.
New York

LARA IN AMERICA

First American Edition, 1977

LC: 77-2486
ISBN: 0-679-20405-9

10 9 8 7 6 5 4 3 2 1

Acknowledgements

To my husband—for all his help and for
providing the incentive for the trip.

Foreword
by H.R.H. The Princess Anne,
Mrs. Mark Phillips, G.C.V.O.

When the British horses travelling to the Ledyard Farm Three Day Event in Massachusetts left the Quarantine Centre in Clifton, New Jersey, they said goodbye to one of their travelling companions on the flight, a Mrs. Adrianne Cooper and her horse Lara. They wished her the best of luck and wondered how she would fare—riding round America.

Now we know Mrs. Cooper fared extremely well and has written an amusing and thoughtful account of her travels. She includes all her preparations and plans and her reasons for her various decisions. She never fails to point out the difficulties involved in taking what she describes as an 'extended holiday in the West'!

What a wonderful thing to have done and how refreshing to read of the hospitality and trust of one's fellow human beings—something one doesn't often hear about. As one of those who went to Ledyard Farm and was present at London Airport at the start of her great adventure, I would like to congratulate Mrs. Cooper and Lara on their achievement and to thank them for the pleasure of being able to read of their success and how they did it.

ANNE

Buckingham Palace
22nd April 1976

Contents

I have deliberately avoided the use of plain and dotted lines to indicate over which parts we trucked and where we rode, as this would be misleading and give no clear idea of the distances involved. Since I avoided large towns and stopped wherever accommodation was available, my route

was, of necessity, circuitous and any attempt to follow it exactly on a small scale map would be impossible. Instead, I have marked in places actually named in the book, and these will, I feel, be sufficient to give the reader a fairly clear idea of where we went.

Lara

Lara, foaled in 1962, was bred by Miss P. Wolf at the Hanstead Stud. She is by the Arab stallion Blue Domino out of a French Anglo-Arab mare, Bethanie II. A copper chestnut, she stands 15·2 hh. high.

I bought her as an eight-year-old from a stud in Derbyshire. Before coming to me she had been shown as a hack, doing well but never quite in the top class, her best achievement being to win the novice championship at the Kent County Show. Her temperament was always against her and she could only be taken to those shows where the judge was known to have light hands. In company, at any speed faster than a walk, she is extremely difficult, lathering up and getting terribly upset if not allowed to go in front. On her own she is a perfect lady—altogether a delightful ride—alert and gay, but sensible. So much so that I can happily ride her bareback with just a headcollar.

In Winter I work—mainly to keep Lara. But I try to arrange to do something with her every Summer. Two years ago we spent five months riding around Ireland, to me the most enchanting and enchanted of lands. Last Summer we were in America. I hope to ride in Eastern Europe, in Hungary, Poland and Czechoslovakia. Otherwise we just potter around Wales, where we have delightful friends and a small tumbledown cottage with a few acres of grazing.

During the rest of the year Lara lives a life of total and well-deserved luxury at Shalbourne Manor, Miss Margeurite de Beaumont's beautiful stud, synonymous with peace and a perfect home for any horse.

Preparation

I JUST WOKE UP one morning and the idea was there. Unconvincing, perhaps, but true. I would fly my horse to the States and ride through the West. In fact I had made a similar trip to Ireland two years ago which proved a tremendous success and must subconsciously have influenced my decision. Also, having reached the psychologically critical age of forty, I was anxious to convince myself of the truth of the adage that Life begins at Forty. Why America? No particular reason, except that I had never been there before.

My husband thoroughly disapproved of the whole venture. A wife's place was at home looking after the family, not gallivanting around. It was irresponsible, selfish and immature. He washed his hands of the whole thing. Actually, a fortnight before zero hour, he suddenly became very helpful and even rushed out to buy me a sewing kit and notebook. Not unnaturally, this caused me to raise a quizzical eyebrow! However he proved to be a tower of strength, as without his added masculine weight I would probably not have been granted a visa and he also very kindly agreed to help with my finances. To fly a horse to America is expensive and the return flight, with its attendant incidental expenses, costs in the region of £2,500. In addition, I took a further £1,000 for out-of-pocket expenses. One might argue that this is a holiday strictly for the rich. I work as a typist and am always short of funds. When all is said and done, it's a question of priorities. Before setting out I managed to save £1,000. The rest I borrowed from a very obliging bank manager and a very obliging husband—mine —to be repaid as soon as possible on my return. In the present economic climate, this arrangement seemed an eminently sensible one.

My son is twenty and my daughter eighteen. Children are always more fair-minded than adults. They want to do their thing and are ready to accord the same privilege to others. Also the pill is sweetened by being able to bask in shades of reflected glory. Basically, their attitude was: if you want to go, go. And the best of British luck! However, judging from the one letter I received from my daughter, sent to Denver Main Post Office for collection if and when I arrived there, my absence was beginning to be felt. The letter finished tersely: 'Shoot the horse, collect the insurance and fly home tomorrow.' My mother, I am sure, missed me very much.

Whilst on the subject of communications, it was agreed that I would from time to time telephone home, reversing the charges, to show that all was well, and the family would refuse to accept the call. If the message was really urgent, I would pay from my end. One such attempt sufficed. I told the operator that Mrs. Cooper was calling collect and wished to speak to Mr. Cooper in London. A pause. 'Mrs. Cooper is on the line calling from the United States. Will you accept the call?' 'No.' 'I beg your pardon?' 'No, I won't accept the call.' A deathly hush and then an obviously very embarrassed operator informed me that the party in London would not accept the call. Mortified, I never telephoned again.

Having decided to go ahead, I wrote to the American Horse Show Association to see whether the idea was actually feasible. The secretary replied, suggesting that I contact a Mrs. Sally O'Connor, who had recently ridden with her two sons from Maryland to Oregon. Sally answered all my queries and proved to be a tower of strength. The last letter I received from her ran as follows:

Preparation

Dear Adrianne,

You worry me a little. In Ireland there are houses and people every ten miles or so, but some of the places you are thinking about over here, you can spend a couple of days miles from nowhere.

Imperative that your horse can be tied or hobbled at some points, as you won't be anywhere near civilisation. It's a very very big country. Its incomprehensible to any English person. I know. I was staggered by the distances out West.

Nebraska has some lovely parts and is a bit more civilised than Wyoming. But Wyoming is so gorgeous that you can't miss it. Nevada and Utah and Arizona are full of desert. And I mean desert. Unless you are an experienced desert traveller, avoid these parts. I routed us through country where I could be sure of water, as I was terrified of being caught out with two kids and three horses. It is bad country. Not like the Sahara, but the heat can be in the hundreds every day and there are often stretches without water for a hundred miles. I mean NO WATER WHATSOEVER. Even stretches of Wyoming and Idaho were pretty grim. As you are doing this as a lark, not trying to get from one side to the other like we did, I think you should be considering how much fun you can have—not how you can survive!

Clothes. Here again, throw out all your English ideas of what is correct, etc. It will be hot and perhaps also terribly cold. Riding breeches or johdpurs are entirely too tight in hot weather. We rode in jeans and chaps, which worked out beautifully. Riding boots are bad in the heat also. We rode in hiking boots, which again worked perfectly. I would strongly advise you to have some sort of loose trousers, otherwise you will get horrible heat rashes, etc. A poncho or slicker is essential for the torrential storms and covers up the horse and saddle more satisfactorily than a riding mac, which again is too bulky and hot. We wore Western hats. A crash cap would give you a terrible headache in the heat. You need a large shady-type hat with a vast brim. We managed without any smart clothes.

Preparation

People figured we were lunatics anyway doing what we were doing and eccentric clothing was accepted as part of us.

Actually out West life is informal all the time and the people are fantastically friendly. I do not think you need to worry about being attacked. The West is funny: women are terribly hardworking and practical types, working as hard as anyone, but the men got very protective towards me. Perhaps the mother and child image or something. But you should not anticipate trouble. New York City— yes; out there—no. I am against guns on principle and reasoned that if I took one, by the time I got it out, loaded, etc., the danger would either be over or have annihilated us. Never did need one.

Dangerous animals. There are some. Rattlesnakes are the worst. We rode right over the top of two, but apart from that, we went our separate ways. There are bears in the high country, but again, if you don't bother them, they will avoid you like the plague. We met one on a mountain path but he ran away, to our relief, I might add. A windproof jacket is essential and a heavy woollen sailing-type sweater for nights up high.

I think you may have to stay in more civilised parts than we tackled. First of all your tethering problem, secondly, oats. You just can't expect a horse to keep going without regular feeding. We carried nosebags and fifty pounds or so of oats at all times and only let the horses down for two meals, which was pretty good going. As long as you stay in habited country, there are plenty of oats available at ranches. Westerners are fiercely hospitable; we had trouble keeping going at times we were so inundated with invitations.

By the way, we carried blacksmith's supplies, etc. The shoeing out West is a bit rough and ready, but it is possible to find competent farriers.

You must seriously consider your horse's back. The extreme heat really tells. The usual saddle pad is not adequate. We wound up with a large pad of four inch foam rubber under everything. Even the two totally unfit horses we borrowed on the way had no back problems with this arrangement. It looks terrible, but it does the job.

I don't know if you can get them in England, but you need VEE, WEE *and* EEE—*Venezuelan, Western and Eastern encephalitis shots for Lara. Also tetanus, etc. It wouldn't do any harm for you to have typhoid. The water we drank out West was the purest I have ever had, but you may as well get the protection in case.*

Well, here are some of the answers. I may be able to manage to drive you out West myself in July. I'm dying to return and see several super people again.

Sally

Although we spoke several times on the telephone, I unfortunately never managed actually to meet Sally whilst I was in America. This was rather sad as, apart from denying me the opportunity of thanking her personally, it would have been interesting to compare our various experiences en route.

In one of her previous letters Sally had mentioned that she and the boys stayed with Ellis Ruby in Nebraska, who had looked after them for several days while they and the horses rested up. She also wrote that only in Nebraska did the riding become interesting, as until then they had been confined almost entirely to tarmac. On the strength of this, I decided that Nebraska would be a sensible jumping-off point and accordingly asked London telephone directory enquiries to find me the address and telephone number of a Mr. Ellis Ruby, who lived in Nebraska, U.S.A.; and to their eternal credit, they promptly did so. I then wrote to Ellis, asking if I might start from his place and, if necessary, rest the mare after her long journey. His reply came by return:

Preparation

Dear Adrianne,

We would be most happy to have you drop in and make this your headquarters. I am not sure just what we can do to help you out but rest assured that all we can do will be done.

We are having a competitive trail ride (thirty-five miles one day and twenty-five the next) on the 21st and 22nd June and you would find that you would meet a lot of interesting people and have a good time if you can be here by that time.

We will be most happy to help you in any way we can.

If you were here a couple of weeks earlier, we would be branding the foals and having our ranch picnic, which is a chance for the ranch men to compete against one another in cutting, roping and other activities.

Hoping to see you in June.

Ellis S. Ruby

This letter, written to a complete and total stranger, typifies the spontaneous and unstinting hospitality of the West.

In the meantime, I checked my tack, had my saddle bags relined, gave in my notice and booked a flight for myself and the horse on the 20th June. At this point, my husband politely mentioned that I had forgotten to apply for a visa. I did so and in due course my application was refused—no reason was given. Armed with indignation and a sheaf of supporting letters, I reapplied, only to meet with the same conspicuous lack of success. So I applied yet again, this time armed with my husband, and hey presto!, I was suddenly the proud possessor of an American visa.

So far, so good. I had a visa, my flight was booked, a starting point had been arranged and I had planned my route to the extent of deciding to head from Nebraska in the general direction of Yellowstone Park. All that remained was to get Lara fit. With this in mind, I took her to Wales and spent the next ten weeks walking and slowly trotting up hill and down dale, gradually increasing her oats and the length of the rides, but never exceeding twenty miles. This produced the desired effect and by the time I took her home, three days before we were due to leave, the mare looked really big and well and was reasonably fit. The local blacksmith very kindly gave me a few basic lessons on shoeing and provided me with an emergency do-it-yourself kit for America, consisting of a spare set of shoes, nails and the lightest possible set of tools. I felt I could probably manage to pull off the old shoes, but lacked faith in my ability to replace them. However, it seemed prudent to take the stuff along. I also practised leading Lara in and out of the trailer, in order to minimise the very real possibility of her refusing to enter the aeroplane and of the flight finally leaving without us.

Nobody, including myself, was taking my proposed trip very seriously. Before leaving Wales, various friends suggested that I acquire a compass, which they assured me would greatly improve my chances of ever finding my way home again. My mother, too, showed a singular lack of faith, by asking me to draw up a suitable document to ensure that, in the event of my disappearing without trace, she be adequately provided for until such time as my will could effectively be proved. Levity notwithstanding, I complied with both suggestions.

My saddle bags are small, but by dint of judicious elimination, I managed to fit in all I needed: a hoof pick, body brush and rubber curry comb; half a bar of glycerine and a rag; an antiseptic spray, lint and a crêpe bandage; several pieces of binder twine and a spare set of reins. So much for the horse. For myself I took one complete change of clothing, consisting of jeans, shirt, socks and underwear;

a pair of shorts, a woolly vest, two handkerchiefs and a pair of plimsolls; a spare pair of spectacles; sunglasses; writing materials; a compass; a penknife; a sewing kit with lots of safety pins; an emergency type sleeping bag, compressed into the size of a cigarette packet; Pushkin's *The Bronze Horseman* in Russian and finally the usual assorted female paraphernalia. Everything was wrapped in plastic bags. I considered taking a spare girth, but the mare has a strong Balding girth and I felt this would last. In addition I took her saddle and bridle and the shoeing kit. I also took a riding mac, a heavy pullover and an anorak, to be tied to the front of the saddle; and having packed all this stuff into two old suit cases, I was ready to go.

I used a standard all-purpose English saddle, referred to in the West as either a pancake or a postage stamp, and a thick plain Egg-butt snaffle bit and a drop noseband. My riding leaves so much to be desired that I felt I could do least damage with this combination. A further point is that, the simpler the bit, the easier it is for a horse to graze, if for some reason it is not practical to remove the bridle altogether. Her tack never made her sore or uncomfortable and she went kindly and quietly in it throughout the trip.

CHAPTER TWO

Journey to Starting Point

JUNE 20TH dawned fair and sunny. At Heathrow airport twenty horses were waiting to be flown out. The majority of these belonged to the British three-day event team, due to compete at Boston: in addition, there were three young event horses, two ponies and Lara. We arrived at the airport at 10.30 a.m. and started loading at 1.00 p.m. We had been asked not to give the horses any food the night before and to bring a full haynet with us. This was given to the horses as soon as they were led into the stalls, in order to distract their attention while the stalls were raised hydraulically to cabin level and then pushed into the aeroplane on rollers. Lara was last in, loading quietly, and we finally took off at 2.15 p.m. There were seventeen passengers, again mostly composed of team members and personnel. The flight was smooth, the atmosphere informal. Champagne flowed and we all helped ourselves to whatever we wanted in the way of food and drink. All the horses travelled quietly and after an uneventful six-and-a-half hours, our DC–6 touched down at Kennedy Airport, taxied slowly across seven miles of runway and finally came to a halt. We had arrived.

Everything at the airport seemed very disorganised. We left the horses to be unloaded and went to customs. An official asked me to open one of my suitcases. 'Which one?' 'Be my guest; the one without the diamonds.' I opened the one without the diamonds. We were then driven by a private bus to immigration. By the time we had all been cleared, the bus had disappeared and it was some considerable time before it could be found again. There were further long delays unloading horses, sorting things out and getting the luggage stowed away. Finally, at 10.30 p.m. New York time we left the airport for the Quarantine Centre at Clifton, New Jersey. It had taken six and a half hours to cross the Atlantic and eight to get away from the airport. When we reached Clifton, the horses' ears and noses were sprayed against bugs and they were then immediately led away to the stables. It was now past midnight, there was nothing more I could do for Lara, and I was very happy to crawl into bed.

It was obvious that I had to get the horse to Nebraska as quickly as possible, since I certainly couldn't afford to stay at Clifton long. The Centre was costing about £12 a day; my motel £8; add a further £10 for food and the total comes to roughly £30 a day. Since I planned to return home early in November, my £500 spending money had to last four and a half months, allowing for a daily expenditure of about £4!

Having established the relative position of the dime and nickel in the hierarchy of the American monetary system, I settled down to telephone—and telephone I did, calling every transport firm listed in the classified directory, by which time it had become abundantly clear that to arrange transport from New Jersey to Nebraska was easier said than done. In theory, there were two possibilities. One could either travel on a van carrying a full complement of horses, in which case the cost would be reasonable: but none of the firms had horses going to the West for at least two weeks— and so far as I was concerned, to wait that long was out of the question. Alternatively, one could arrange for a van to come immediately and travel with only the one horse; but this would cost nearly £1,000, which was obviously even more out of the question.

Discouraged, I went to the Centre, where they refused to let me see Lara. A great pile of disinfected rugs, bandages, etc., was waiting to be sorted out. My leg bandages turned up, but the tail bandage was missing—the first of a long line of articles which I was to leave strewn across the States. These included, in chronological order, a pullover, an anorak, a silver ring, a hoof pick, a penknife, my precious Pushkin and finally a $35 hat. I helped load the team horses, which had finally been cleared, and after wishing each other mutual good luck, the team left and I was on my own.

Back at the motel, I telephoned Sally. She suggested I contact Mike Grady, who is in the horse transport business and whom she highly recommended. Nebraska was out of his territory, but he gave me the name of a firm out West. Several hours and telephone calls later, we had arranged that they would pick up the horse at Lexington, Kentucky, at 12.00 p.m. on Tuesday, take her on to Omaha, where arrangements would be made for another van to take her on to her final destination. So far, so good. Back and forth to Mike again, who promised to have a van at the Centre at 3.00 p.m. on Monday, to reach Lexington in time to make the connection. The near impossible had been achieved and I celebrated by treating myself to an enormous steak. These arrangements were, in fact, very satisfactory: we were setting out with a minimum of delay and the cost was very reasonable.

It was amusing to find that so many of the things one hears about America were true. The steaks are excellent; so is the ice-cream. People really do smoke big fat cigars, drive enormous cars and say Jesus Kerrist. I personally very much appreciated being given a glass of liberally iced water with every meal as a matter of course, and also the pleasantness with which one was invariably served. Salads in America struck me as being particularly good, coffee particularly bad. Everyone was very friendly. These initial impressions remained true wherever I went, with the exception of New York, which is in any case a law unto itself.

I arrived at the Centre promptly at 2.30 p.m. so as to have

time to lead Lara around and give her a chance to stretch her legs before the eight hundred mile journey ahead to Lexington. As it turned out, I needn't have worried, since the van only arrived at 5.00 p.m. and this lack of punctuality —give or take a few hours—proved to be typical of every van I travelled on subsequently. Six horses were travelling. The three boys in charge put Lara, who was in season, next to a stallion. I insisted she be moved, made sure she had plenty of bedding and a full hay-net, and we were off. Generally speaking, a horse is better off if the owner is there to see to its comfort and I always rode in the back with Lara until I was sure that she had settled down and was travelling quietly.

The journey was marred by the regular monotony with which we kept breaking down—to be precise, five times in fairly rapid succession. At night, we would pull off the interstate, flares would be set up, a lengthy consultation would be held, a breakdown van called and we would ignominiously be towed into the bowels of some garage. During the day it was worse, as the temperature was well up in the nineties and as soon as the van stopped for any length of time the heat inside rapidly began to build up. I felt very sorry for the horses. However, all bad things must come to an end and we finally reached Lexington at 6.00 p.m., seven hours late.

As though on cue the other van, presumably also seven hours late, arrived within five minutes. The drivers, as was nearly always the case, insisted on loading the horses themselves. At the slightest sign of difficulty they became rough and impatient, with the result that Lara finally had to be backed in. I could never persuade them to let me do the job myself and so avoid all the fuss and excitement. However, once away from the horses, they were invariably charming and I very much enjoyed their company. Travelling for any long distance on these vans soon becomes tiring. There is a sleeping compartment behind the front seats, partitioned off by a curtain, where the drivers take turns to sleep, and I often used this for a catnap. Once I slept on some hay in the back; another time, more luxuriously, in a sleeping bag; but it was difficult really to rest and this difficulty was aggravated by the noise. Two-way radios are standard equipment and are constantly being used, both for ordinary conversational purposes and to warn other drivers of police hazards ahead. The Chief Constable of, I believe, Missouri, is referred to as Smokey Bear No. 1. I never understood a word that was being said due to the terrible static, but apparently you get used to it. These vans ride extremely smoothly, an average speed of seventy miles an hour is maintained and most of the drivers are excellent. We had already crossed Pennsylvania, Ohio and Kentucky. Now we roared through Indiana, Illinois, Missouri, Kansas and Iowa, dropping horses en route, before finally reaching Omaha, in Nebraska, at seven o'clock on Wednesday evening. Here we were let off to spend the night at a racing stable and to await a van to cover the last 400 miles or so to western Nebraska the following morning.

After the long journey, it was nice to be greeted with: 'Would you like her put on sawdust or on straw?' The stables were cool and free from flies. There was a choice of alfalfa or timothy hay. Lara was given a feed and left to rest. I was astonished, even allowing for the fact that we had been travelling non-stop for fifty hours, at the amount of condition she had lost. However, all through the trip she would not only lose, but also gain weight with amazing rapidity, often literally from day to day, and I have since been told that this is a typically Arab trait.

The owner of the stables kindly offered to drive me to a motel, but Marcy, who helps to run the place, said that she would gladly put me up if I didn't mind sharing her little flat, so that I could be near the horse. We ate supper and I had my first taste of sweet potatoes, which were delicious. I was later to be introduced to the gastronomic delights of buffalo, moose, antelope, squirrel and beef jerky; of banana bread, shoefly pie, choke cherry syrup and apricot leather; of moonshine and rattlesnake. Unfortunately, I never tasted bear.

Next day a reporter telephoned to ask for an interview and duly arrived with a photographer. This was my first experience of being interviewed in the States—or anywhere else for that matter—and I found the situation vaguely embarrassing, particularly as I did not feel that I had done anything to merit attention. However, to a small local paper presumably any news is better than no news and it would have been churlish to refuse. As the trip progressed, I was 'written up' so often that I developed into a blasé interviewee.

The results of a write-up were sometimes helpful, sometimes amusing, always touching. On one occasion, I was riding along, quietly minding my own business, when a car roared up and screeched to a dramatic halt. Fully prepared to be annoyed at such inconsiderate behaviour, I was totally disarmed when a dear old lady jumped out, rushed up and said that she had read about me in the paper: she so much wanted to shake me by the hand and wish me luck and to be able to say that she had met me!

Another time, after a really long and tiring ride, we came to a livery barn. The place was unlocked and I led Lara in. All the boxes were full, with the exception of one large one at the end. This was beautifully bedded down with clean

Lara

Lara at the Arab show, ridden by Deirdre Robinson, where she came Reserve

Lara at home

straw, there was plenty of hay, fresh water and a feed in the manger—very much like Goldilocks and the three bears, in fact. Nobody was about, so I took a chance and put Lara in. Then I settled down to wait. About two hours later the owner turned up and welcomed me literally with open arms. He had read about me in the paper, he said, and judging from the route I was taking knew I would be heading this way. On the off-chance that I might stop at his barn, he had kept a box prepared so that it would be ready when I arrived! To be expected is always nice; but to be expected when you yourself don't even know you are coming is little short of miraculous.

People were constantly stopping me on the road to ask if I was the Englishwoman they had read about. It wasn't just idle curiosity. Everyone wanted to help. A bar of chocolate or a packet of sweets would be produced and slipped into my saddle bag—'Just in case you get hungry'. If the person happened to live close by, I was asked to stop for a drink or a meal, to 'give the horse a chance to rest'. Lorry drivers would pull over, produce a thermos and we would chat over a mug of coffee and a cigarette. These impromptu meetings, whilst slowing down one's rate of progress, made it infinitely more enjoyable.

Some of the local papers had wonderful names—for example, the *Caribou County Sun*—so much more fun than *The Times*. In fact, throughout the West, I was enchanted by the place names. Those of Indian origin were beautifully melodious: Shoshone National Forest; Rawah Wilderness; Yampa River. (Yampa means bear and is, I think, a splendid word). Simple names like Shawnee, Arapaho, Cheyenne. Those vividly evoking the trials and tribulations of the early settlers: Skull Valley, Thunder Basin, Wagon Wheel Gap; Cache Poudre Canyon, Gunfight Pass; Spotted Horse

Gulch, Skinny Fish Lake. On a lighter note, in Pennsylvania I stayed at a place situated between two small towns—Bird-in-Hand and Intercourse.

However, I digress. After the interview, I took Marcy out to lunch and we looked round the Omaha shopping centre, the eighth largest in the world. Marcy, who, incidentally, is a very young looking grandmother, showed me all her Western outfits, of which she has cupboards full, and a most beautiful Western saddle and bridle. Small and slender, she looked perfect in her Western clothes, the high-heeled boots providing just the right touch of added height. She was never short of admirers and regularly graced the local hops. But Marcy was more than just a pretty face and her store of energy was apparently inexhaustible. No doubt the blood of the pioneers still flowed strongly in her veins. Every morning she was up at four; she fed, watered and mucked out fifteen horses; she drove the muck-spreader straight out into the fields and disposed of the contents; a short pause for breakfast and then she strapped till lunch; a couple of hours off, then back to work, often not finishing till after eight. Her work was done with pride and it was done cheerfully. The standards she maintained were such as have all but died out in England and are in any case only remembered by a few old-timers. Nor, I hasten to add, were they in any way typical of the West. Marcy was extraordinarily generous and was most disappointed when I refused to accept a really lovely fringed pair of Western gloves and a small portable radio to entertain me whilst riding along! However, I gladly took a silver dollar for luck.

The van was due to come at 7.00 p.m. and promptly (for a van) at 7.30 p.m. it arrived. Everyone wished me luck and we were off once more. I hated to say goodbye. Leaving friends is always sad, the more so when the future is uncertain. But I realised that this was an unavoidable aspect of the trip, the conflicting strands an integral part of its fabric.

CHAPTER THREE

The West

WE DROVE STEADILY all night and arrived at Ellis Ruby's place at seven the next morning. Our unheralded arrival was accepted as a matter of course. Lara was put into a corral, with access to a forty acre field, with two yearlings and a five-year-old gelding. This was the first and last time during the whole trip that I turned her out with strange horses: but I didn't like to argue and as it turned out, no damage was done.

Ellis was a tall, pleasant-looking man to whom one was instinctively drawn. He had that rare quality of effortless authority, a combination of personality and competence, which inspired immediate confidence. A gentle man, everything about him was relaxed, unhurried—his slow smile, his drawling speech, his loose movements; yet such was their economy and precision that not a moment was ever wasted. After breakfast I was driven round the ranch, where Arabs are bred and broken for use on other ranches within the same organisation. Everything struck me as vast. In Nebraska there are single fields of more than a thousand acres. When the land is poor, sixty acres per horse is considered reasonable. I was privileged, and I use the word advisedly, to watch Ellis training the two-year-olds. They had only been backed a week or so ago but were already extremely handy at the walk, trot and canter; were neck-reining nicely and coping with elementary lateral work. Not many ranches use pure-bred Arabs for working the cattle, preferring the quarter horse: but Ellis maintained that an Arab was equal, if not superior, to a quarter horse for all aspects of ranch work, with the possible exception of being a shade light when it came to roping a heavy steer, but even here it was largely a question of correctly position-ing the horse in relation to the steer. Although Ellis never mentioned the fact, I later learned that he had a Ph.D in genetics. This put him among that rare and happy band of men living in surroundings and doing work which they not only love, but for which their specialist and practical training ideally fits them.

We had lunch in town and met several of Ellis's friends, who obviously thought I was completely mad; back home to meet Ellis's mother; off to another town to buy some things for myself and the horse; out to drinks with more friends; home to dinner. It occurred to me that if this pattern was to be typical of the rest of the trip, I wouldn't last a fortnight. In fact, it was typical. Wherever I went, people would go out of their way to introduce me to friends and relatives and to show me the local sights: and surprising-ly, I not only survived but obviously thrived on it, as I returned home looking better than ever before and feeling ten years younger.

At Ellis's suggestion I acquired, for the astronomical sum of $35.00, a Western hat. This looked absolutely stunning, but proved to be a mixed blessing: in hot weather, one sweated profusely; in the wind, it immediately blew off; and as I was never bothered by either rain or sun, I was able to bear its eventual loss with equanimity. The last I saw of it, on a particularly gusty day and several states later, was bobbing merrily away down the river. I was also advised to buy an excellent saddle pad; a lariat, in case Lara needed to be tethered or pulled out of a swamp—I was never really sure exactly for what—but it looked great and I attached it to my English 'postage stamp' and hoped the incongruity would pass unnoticed; a much longer headcollar rope, far more convenient for holding her while she grazed; and finally two sets of rawhide thongs to replace the shoelaces with which I had tied everything to the saddle.

Ellis very generously told me that if anything went wrong with Lara, he would be happy to lend me one of his horses for the rest of the trip and would get it to me wherever I was—I had only to let him know. He also telephoned ahead to arrange my first two stops and gave me a few additional names along the route. This was a tremendous help, as it was always a great relief to know that when you arrived somebody would be expecting you.

If no such arrangements had been made, there was nothing for it but to ride on and hope for the best; but it was prudent first to make sure that there were suitable ranches along the route. I didn't particularly mind asking for accommodation for the horse and naturally always offered to pay for anything she had, but I lacked the temerity to ask for myself. The only alternative, since obviously I had to sleep somewhere, was to suggest staying with the horse. I was never happy about this as I felt that, in a backhanded way, people were being put on the spot, but I honestly didn't know what else to do. Usually they insisted at once that I stay with them and, to their eternal credit, seemed really delighted at the prospect. Once or twice I did end up in the barn.

Only once did I come completely unstuck. We had to cross a certain pass and it was forty miles to the other side. I was assured by several people that about half way over there was an old German prisoner-of-war camp. The prisoners used to work in the forest and had been supervised on horseback. The stables and buildings were still standing, there was plenty of wood for heating and I could arrange about food when I arrived. This didn't sound too promising, but since beggars can't be choosers, I sallied forth. Presently

I began to make tentative enquiries as to the exact where-
abouts of my proposed night's lodging. 'Prisoner-of-war
camp? What prisoner-of-war camp?' Nobody had the
faintest idea what I was talking about. There was no
question of riding on for another twenty-five miles as it was
getting late and I didn't want to be caught in the dark. So
I turned off the main track and followed a smaller one
towards, I hoped, a dude ranch, which I had been told was
a few miles further on. Dusk was falling; the temperature
was falling; my courage was falling. We were absolutely
alone and I thought longingly of the friendly ranch lights
twinkling just around the next corner . . . and the next . . .
and the next . . . Suddenly I heard a whinny; Lara stepped
out. In fact there were five horses in a small corral. Obviously I couldn't put Lara in with them and there were no other
buildings except a caravan and a trailer house, both apparently deserted. Just outside the corral were stacked about
fifty bales of hay. I tied Lara to one of these, took her tack
off, brushed her over and gave her water from the trough.
Hay she had in plenty. Fortunately it was excellent and she
tucked in with gusto. Presently a young man turned up. He
lived in the caravan and worked there. The owners might or
might not come back tonight. First he produced an enormous feed for Lara. She ate it all up so we gave her a second
helping. I had a preliminary cup of coffee while my new-
found friend made supper, which we ate al fresco, sitting on
the bales. The dude ranch, he told me, did in fact exist, but
was another ten miles on down the road. The temperature
was already below freezing and it was with regret that I
declined the amenities of the caravan, but I didn't dare
leave Lara on her own. I borrowed three blankets—one of
which I put on Lara—and settled down to sleep. It was a
beautiful clear night, a happy night with enormous twink-

ling stars. I must have dozed off despite the cold because something woke me. Lara, standing on three legs—apparently as happily as on four—was nudging me. She had been pawing and her shoe was firmly caught in the wire round one of the bales. I fumbled round in the dark and eventually managed to free her. All the time she never so much as twitched an ear and as soon as I was finished went straight back to munching hay. I awoke early and the owners, who had returned some time during the night, rushed me into the house, insisted that I have a hot bath, plied me with scalding coffee and an enormous breakfast and only then was I permitted to go on my way. This was the only time during the whole trip that I slept in the open and I thoroughly enjoyed it.

In one of the National Parks I slept under a fire engine. A ranger kindly offered me his caravan, but I didn't want to be a nuisance and gratefully accepted the loan of a sleeping bag instead. Lara had a very nice corral with grass and pine trees and in the evening I settled down with her. Or rather I tried to settle down. It poured with rain; the mosquitoes were out in force and Lara never stopped walking round and round. Finally, in desperation, I dragged my sleeping bag and other bits and pieces to the fire cache, the only building within miles, where all the fire engines were kept. A friend, who for obvious reasons shall be nameless, had kindly left the lavatory door at the back unlocked. This was against all the rules and I had promised, if I used the place, to lock up and be out before the men arrived for work next day. I pulled my sleeping bag under a fire engine, and hoping there wouldn't be a fire in the night, dozed off. The sound of cars awoke me. It was two o'clock. The lights clicked on and suddenly the place was full of people. I shut my eyes and pretended to be fast asleep.

Footsteps came and paused and went. Voices were lowered and receded. Eventually the lights went off, the cars went off and, pausing only long enough to lock the door, I too went off. It wasn't funny—not at my age—just humiliating. And for the first time I felt like a real bum.

If I happened to be in a town, I stayed at a motel. There was no problem with the horse as every town in the West has a rodeo ground, which in turn has very adequate stabling facilities. I always enjoyed the motels, firstly because they were very clean and comfortable and secondly because I could let my hair down and completely relax. No matter how great the kindness I was shown—and nothing I can say can do it justice—it was still a strain, even if only a subconscious one—always to be facing strangers, feeling one's way and being the centre of attention.

Throughout the trip I kept a diary or, to be more precise, I jotted down in an old exercise book brief notes on the day's events. I reproduce below (with apologies for literary lacunae) my notes on the first four days' riding since, with the exception of what appears to be an inordinate amount of trucking, they are in many respects typical of the rest of the journey.

28.6.1975. Up at 4.30 to pack saddle bags and generally sort myself out. Decided to leave shoeing stuff behind. Too inexperienced, too heavy and anyway no room. Will take all travellers cheques with me, but not passport. Had coffee with Ellis and he rode with me to end of his land and put me on road for Stop No. 1. Set out at 7.00. Reached destination—twenty-two miles—with one hour's rest. Roads here lovely for riding—sand and gravel. Very soft but not too dusty. Walked right over first snake and only noticed it when half way over. Water snake. Next one we came across a Bull snake. Lara couldn't care less. Rested, after checking for rattle-

snakes, in only bit of shade under tree. Very hot by 10.00, well into nineties. Lara sweating a lot but going well and seems quite happy. I look like a real cowgirl—my hat is beautiful and very smart and my 'rope' looks good. Arrived at 1.00. Charming couple with two lovely kids. Really happy home. Put Lara into stable. Gave her loads of hay (for bedding as well) and big feed of corn and oats, which she didn't touch. Beautiful house, my room all ready. Had shower. Worse luck no one offered me anything to eat, so just starved. Cleaned Lara up. Drove round farm—24,000 acres. Watched cows being artificially inseminated. All very interesting. Did Lara up for night. Had dinner—pizza and salad. Too embarrassed to have more than three slices, although dying for more. The children charming—six and nine—and have ideal life. Ride out with father to check cattle, have baby calves, puppies, freedom. Boy drives pick-up and both ride in back and no one worries. Was given detailed plan of how to get to next place. Only fourteen miles away, but seven over open country with only tracks. Bed at 9.30. Said I would slip out quietly at 5.00, so as to ride in cool and avoid awful mosquitoes and horse flies. Lara all in lumps and bumps from yesterday. Didn't pay for anything except packet of cigarettes, which they let me buy, as I had run out. Really, really nice, gentle, kind family.

29.6.1975. Up at 4.30, ready to go at 5.30. Got as far as first windmill (everywhere for water) and couldn't sort out which track I was supposed to follow. So before I got lost in 24,000 acres without a landmark in sight, just came back home. Put Lara back in stable. Returned to house at 6.00 and waited till 7.30 for someone to wake up. Explained my predicament. Completely understood and tactfully said even native might well have got lost and surprised I had been sent that way and best thing to return. We agreed he would take Lara by trailer to road part of ride. So we loaded up and eventually set off at 9.30. How kind people are! Soon realised I had left sweater and anorak behind, but luckily had transferred travellers cheques to saddle bags. This ride spoiled:

(*a*) *by heat, although wind blowing;*

(*b*) *by hundreds of wire gates, which are a bloody nuisance to say least—cut my finger on one and it bled like mad;*

(*c*) *my hat blowing off. In the end had to hold it all the time. Arrived at Moss's place at 12.30. Very slow going indeed. Again, wonderful people. Older, with twenty-two grandchildren already. Put Lara into cool barn, gave her big feed of oats and hay and left her to dry off. Mr. Moss helped with everything. Then came into lunch. Super one and, thank God, encouraged to eat a lot, but I never eat as much as I would like. Cleaned Lara up. Met parents and son. All these families seem so happy and 'together'—lovely atmosphere. Took me to see stud of quarter horses and then drove to see herd of buffalo. Home at 9.00. Bedded Lara down on hay— again no straw—fed her, etc. Mr. Moss helped. Agreed to take her in trailer first ten miles and will ride last twenty. Arranged to be up at 4.00, so as to beat weather. Also planned route and made map. Had bath and chocolate cake and ice cream and am now going to bed. Will clean tack tomorrow. Lara really settling down and contented. Gave me almost new tin of spray against flies. Extra- ordinary kindness and do feel that I am liked, not just tolerated. Bed now at 10.00.*

30.6.1975. Up at 4.00. Mrs. Moss very kindly got up to see I had good breakfast—bacon, eggs, orange juice, coffee, etc. Then Mr. Moss drove me ten miles or so to starting point for ride. So kind, as busy man; very careful and really gentle and sweet with horses. I was sorry to leave them and they to see me go. Did twenty miles O.K. Arrived, after losing my way at end about four times and adding at least five miles to journey. Boiling hot, no wind at all. At last found place and couldn't open wire gate as too stiff. So waited for passing car—1½ hours—and woman helped and together we managed to fix it. Then rode on to next cattle grid and couldn't find wire gate at all. So went back to first cattle grid and waited another two hours for next car. Stopped it and told them my trouble. They went to fetch

Alinfords, who came soon after. Had been four hours in boiling hot sun. Felt awful and depressed and sorry for Lara. She wouldn't eat rubbishy grass. When cross, take it out on her and she is so good and sweet. Rode on two miles to house. Put Lara in. Kids all fetched things for her—oats, hay, water, etc. Was given big meal and iced lemonade. Place full of trophies for riding. Wife particularly sweet and soon felt better—but not for long as no one knew where I could go next. Wheat country and no horses, no grass, no nothing. Wish I'd never come. Lara seems sad. Had a sleep, as dead tired. Then saw to Lara and stayed to talk to her to try and cheer her up. Supper. Wanted to buy cigarettes off one of the men, but refused to take money. Some friends came over to see if they could think of somewhere for me to sleep tomorrow, but no luck. Took details for local paper. Bed at 11.00. Wish we were back home—and when I think of having to arrange and co-ordinate journey home, feel sick. Bad enough getting here.

1.7.1975. Slept well. Up at 6.00. Gave Lara more feed, as actually ate up. Breakfast. More telephone calls about where I should go and finally something sorted out. Will go by trailer about thirty miles and ride twenty or so. Had awful job loading her, as trailer very narrow. . . . We are now in Alliance, waiting for vet (who is operating on bull to mend broken shaft—interesting, but couldn't watch long as smell of blood too sickly) to give Lara sleeping sickness and 'flu shots. These people have been to endless trouble—dozens of 'phone calls and long trailer ride. Feeling a bit more cheerful now. Dropped me by vast dam and rode last twenty miles. Very hot and Lara not going well at end. Mrs. Tollman waiting for me. Immediately sat me down on deck chair and fetched iced tea and cookies, while I held Lara. Then we went to barn on son's place, about two miles away, and I put Lara in. Gave her hay, water and oats, which she didn't eat. Then back to mother's place. She is psychic or best hostess in world. Everything I thought of that I needed she came out with first—bath, cold drinks, clothes washed.

Had beautiful bedroom all ready. Bathed and washed hair. Clothes done in machine. Then son, Buzz, and husband came and we worked out our route for tomorrow. Delicious dinner. Obviously Mrs. Tollman had gone to enormous amount of trouble on my behalf. Decided easier if I slept at Buzz's place, so as to be near horse for early start tomorrow. Mixed bran with oats in hope she would eat up, but no good. Gave me free rodeo tickets for three days of local rodeo. Begged me to stay on for that period—2nd, 3rd and 4th— but felt I should press on. Slept in basement. Wanted to wait up for wife, who was decorating float for 4th July parade, but too tired. Quite a lot of tornado damage round here and place a bit of a mess...

So much for my diary.

I was struck by the happy atmosphere of the homes in which I stayed. There was no trace of the matriarchal society which I had been led to believe existed in America. On the contrary, this was still very much a man's world: his job was to provide; a woman's to stay at home and look after him. Little words like please and thank you were often conspicuous by their absence, but the women seemed perfectly satisfied with the status quo. The vast majority were excellent housewives. Bread was baked at home as a matter of course; shelves gleamed with serried ranks of home-made pickles, preserves and jellies. Beautiful quilting was done, keeping alive the traditional patterns. And these same women could, with equal ease, skin and prepare an animal for the deep freeze. They could drive a tractor, milk a cow and were prepared, if necessary, to work sixteen hours a day alongside their menfolk.

In the face of such efficiency, I felt quite guilty and resolved to bottle and pickle like mad when I got home— but drew the line at quilting. On one occasion, I was forced to conclude that, not only was I inefficient, but also ineffec-

Lara in Wyoming; Idaho; Colorado and Kentucky

On the road

Marcy   Hesse the mule man

tual. I happened to be with some friends at a rodeo and they asked me to take the children home and baby sit, while they went out to dinner. A simple enough request, one might think, by any standards. But no: I was nervous of driving alone with two small children and a baby; it was night time and I can't see in the dark; the car had automatic transmission, with which I was unfamiliar; a valuable roping horse had to be towed home, and I had never driven with a trailer; I would have had to drive on the wrong side of the road; I wasn't sure of the way; and to cap it all, I had no licence. I did baby sit, but only after first having been ignominiously driven home.

Nor, as I had been led to believe, were American children obnoxious brats. With one or two exceptions, they were absolutely charming with naturally good manners and a real pleasure to be with. In the free and easy atmosphere of the ranch, the children were treated with great tolerance. At an early age, the boys could hunt, shoot and fish; they could take a four-wheel drive up the most precipitous slopes; they helped to round up sheep, drive cattle and bring in the horses. All this activity not only helped to keep them out of mischief, but developed a close and satisfying relationship between father and son. One mother told me that, as a ten-year-old, when she rode to school with her younger sister, they were expected to kill all rattlesnakes they came across and did so as a matter of course.

A brief word of explanation about wire gates, which were ubiquitous throughout the West and proved to be a terrible nuisance. A six foot section or so of the fence could be unhooked at the top and bottom from the supporting upright and rolled back to allow plenty of room for stock to be driven through, and every cattle grid had a corresponding wire gate. These were invariably made of barbed wire and herculean strength was needed to open, let alone to close them. I soon developed a very unpioneer-like attitude! Whenever I knew that a lot of these gates were going to have to be faced next day, I tried to organise a 'dress rehearsal'. This entailed going for a dummy run in the car and checking every single wire gate to make sure I could open it. On one such expedition, there were at least twenty gates with which I could never have coped had I been on my own.

The road to Fort Robinson winds through pine woods with high sandstone buttes on either side. This is real Indian country, rugged and wild, and the Fort itself is an old cavalry post used for training remounts at the height of the Indian troubles. It has two fascinating museums, which document in great detail the early life style of the Indians and the various campaigns fought in the vicinity. All the original buildings and tools at the Fort are carefully preserved: the old blacksmith's shop, the wheelwright's shop, the gun and locksmiths' shops, the parade grounds, the stables with boxes for some two hundred horses—no accommodation problems here for Lara. One could easily imagine the horses galloping in, dust flying, bugles blowing and somewhere, hidden by the surrounding buttes, silently approaching, the Indians. . . . All of this has been very cleverly combined with a flourishing commercial side. The officers' quarters have been converted into a hotel and several additional chalets are dotted about the extensive grounds. All the usual dude-ranch type attractions have been laid on; hay rides, cook-outs, sing-songs and the place was deservedly popular. Several thousands of acres, supporting a wide variety of wild life, both bird and animal —not to mention innumerable snakes—also belong to the Fort: and all this is the direct responsibility of the superintendent. Tall and very good looking, slightly stooped and with the suggestion of an incipient smile always on his lips, Vincent Rotherham was very much in evidence, keeping an eye on his domain. The week I was there was particularly busy, as it was rodeo time and there was also an exhibition of Western art and sculpture being held at the hotel. In view of this, it was especially kind of him and his wife to devote so much time to me, and they did all they could to make my stay enjoyable. I was driven to see herds of buffalo and antelope. We looked at Toadstool Park, an area of incredible mushroom-shaped formations, the result of centuries of erosion. We went to see a buffalo kill-site, where the Indians used to drive thousands of buffalo over the edge of the cliff and all the tribes would briefly gather to partake of the spoil; nothing was wasted and only the bones remained in silent witness to the carnage.

The first night of the rodeo was childrens' night and great fun. Little tots, almost buried under enormous Stetsons, strode around looking for all the world like miniature editions of their fathers. They were absolutely fearless and and even five-year-olds rode the bucking calves. Everyone galloped around like bats out of hell and seemed thoroughly to enjoy themselves.

The following night, the Rotherhams took me to see my first 'real' rodeo. Later I went to many more and was fortunate enough almost always to be taken by actual competitors, who were able to explain the finer points of the various events. One of the things I learned was always to watch from the chutes, as this makes the whole thing much more exciting. Whilst I admired the skill and courage of the calf ropers, the bulldoggers and the bronc and bull riders, I enjoyed the cutting events the most, because there was absolutely no element of cruelty involved. The speed and intelligence with which these horses went about their work was fascinating to watch and one was left with the impression that all the rider had to do was to sit tight, give the horse plenty of rein and interfere as little as possible.

During the rodeo, the loudspeaker asked for Mrs. Adrianne Cooper to go to the announcer's booth. I wondered what I had done, but it was only Ellis, wanting to make sure I had arrived safely. He introduced me to Dr. Bill Munson, with whom I was to stay, and I felt very lucky to be surrounded by so many friends. Buzz was also at the rodeo and asked if I would mind being introduced to the crowd. Feeling a spoil-sport, I declined—just as on subsequent occasions I declined to ride in rodeo parades, largely from fear of falling off or otherwise making a fool of myself in front of such a large audience.

I had spent three eventful days at Fort Robinson and it was time to move on. Now cacti of various types began to mingle with the wild flowers; gophers and chipmunks scurried through the sand; the Yucca plant, used long ago for making soap, stood sentinel by the roadside and the badlands, strangely scarred and fissured, lay ahead. In these unlikely surroundings I came upon a veritable Garden of Eden, an oasis lying in the wilderness: a house, surrounded by fragrant pine trees, where cattle grazed and wild turkey roosted; where fruit and vegetables grew in joyous abundance; where the creek was filled with trout and turtles basked in the shallows. And in these delightful surroundings I whiled away the hours until it was time to leave next day.

Dr. Bill Munson is one of the foremost experts in the United States on Arabs and their breeding. He is pursuing a very interesting and unusual programme of in-breeding, which has already reached the seventh generation and which he hopes to continue to the tenth. His horses are 56% inbred and so far show absolutely no ill effects, either in conformation or temperament. He very kindly drove me round his beautiful ranch, where he keeps about one hundred and seventy Arab horses, and those I saw were small and true to type with very fine heads and great width between the jawbones. He compared an Arab to a camel, meaning, I assume, that if a camel's back end was good enough for the work it had to do, then so was an Arab's.

Some two hundred miles or so of flat and desolate sagebrush lay ahead and I had no intention of wasting time riding across it. Dr. Munson lent me one of his trailers and arranged for a friend to drive me, which was particularly kind as haymaking was in full swing. At Dubois, after exhaustive enquiries, the prognosis was glum. No horses, I was told, were allowed into Yellowstone Park; there were absolutely no stopping places on the way; I would surely get lost; there would be no food, no help available. I did fleetingly wonder whether it wouldn't be wiser just to go back with the trailer while I still had the chance; but since the source of all these dire predictions was a local guide, I felt he might be trying to frighten me into paying for his services, and decided to push on.

There was only one possible place suitable for the horse in Dubois and I was lucky to find it. In fact the stables were still being built, but Lara had a roof over her head, which was all that mattered. The McGregors' house was the most modern I have ever seen. The bathroom taps were of such an exceedingly strange design that I ended up by having a cold bath and cleaning my teeth with hot water! There was radio communication and television in every room, including the bathrooms, and I suppose I could have radioed for advice—had I known how to do so. Mr. McGregor was the best steak cook one could wish to meet and I shall long remember the enormous, succulent, garlic-flavoured steak which he placed in front of me. So often people would afford me a glimpse of their deep-freeze, groaning with home-butchered beef, only to shut the door, casually remarking that they were fed up with steaks, and serve something else. I could have wept.

Travelling through this part of Wyoming was difficult, but I always managed to find somewhere to stay. At one place, since Lara's shoes were very badly worn, one of the ranch hands kindly offered to put on another set, and really it was a case of Hobson's choice. Within a week or so, her near hind hoof had split from the coronet down and she started knocking herself behind. Fortunately, no damage was done, but this experience taught me never to have her shod by anyone other than a qualified farrier. Almost everyone in the West who had anything at all to do with horses considered himself competent to 'bang on' a set of shoes. In fact, due to ignorance and neglect, the state of many horses' feet was shocking. Nearly all shoeing was done cold and many horses had to be cast before they could be shod. Lara's shoes lasted about one hundred and fifty to two hundred miles. Unfortunately I was only told about Boreum at the end of my trip. This is a very hard substance which is welded on to the shoe and makes a set last three or four times as long. Had I known earlier, I could have saved myself a lot of money, although several blacksmiths, with characteristic American generosity, refused to accept any payment for their work, which was 'their contribution to the trip'.

Our most beautiful ride was in Wyoming. The road wound upwards through magnificent pine woods; clear rushing streams tumbled over rocks and cascaded down sheer granite; there were glassy mountain lakes and meadows carpeted with wild flowers; and everything was framed by the towering, snow-capped Tetons. We stopped to rest and watched a fawn graze nearby; a moose, surprisingly graceful, trotted past; a bear stood watching on the slope above. Snow still lay in patches on the ground, and the air was crisp and fresh, filled with the moist scent of earth and pine. We were here alone, and this was our reward for coming.

We rode through the Teton National Park and stopped at Flagg Ranch, a mile or so from Yellowstone. I had hoped to enter the park through the South Gate, ride out through the West Gate and so into Montana. I could then decide whether to go on up towards Canada, possibly through Oregon and Washington, or down towards Idaho and Utah. As it turned out, I could have taken the horse through the park had I been willing to camp out, but for my purposes, suitable places to stay were too few and far between. The decision had been taken out of my hands. I turned sharp left for Idaho. Before leaving, however, I went on a bus tour of the park. This proved to be a great disappointment—especially Old Faithful. Bears were so thin on the ground that nobody I met had ever seen one. In fact, due to the stupidity of the public, they had had to be whisked out of the park by helicopter, so as thoroughly to disorientate them, and then to be deposited in lonely places, far from the madding crowd.

My first stop in Idaho didn't look too promising. We had a beautiful ride through pine woods, but the going was very stony and at the end of twenty-five miles, we had both had enough. The one and only ranch within miles was an awful place, recently bought by a couple from the city, whose unfriendly attitude came as a shock after the kindness of the local people. There was only one corral, full of rocks and boulders, with no shelter, no hay, no oats. A scummy-looking lake nearby, however, ensured a plentiful supply of mosquitoes. I now noticed for the first time the crack in Lara's hoof. All I had was my No. 7 Boots face cream (enriched with lanolin) and I rubbed this liberally into her hoofs and smothered the rest of her with bug spray. Then I set off to find some food. I got a lift at once and explained my predicament. Perhaps I looked hungry, as the driver first of all gave me cookies and iced tea and then tried to contact one of the forest rangers on his two-way radio, but without success. So we drove on until we came to a group of men loading horses on to a pick-up. I changed vehicles and in no time at all had been driven to a house where, they said, I would be most welcome to stay tomorrow; a pile of sweet-smelling hay was collected from a field and a bucket of oats provided. One of the men, Hesse, drove me back and helped me to feed Lara. He then asked me to come and have supper with his friends. About twenty people were gathered round a blazing camp fire; horses and mules stood tethered nearby. We ate moose and drank punch and toasted marshmallows. We talked and laughed and passed the whisky round. And what had promised to be a disastrous evening turned into a lovely one, full of warmth and friendship.

Hesse was known to everyone as 'Hesse, the mule man'. Pale-faced beneath on enormous Stetson, tall and slender, he reminded me of a velvet-headed mushroom striving to reach the forest-filtered sunlight. There was about him an air of melancholy, an underlying sadness, which even the warmth of his impulsive nature could not entirely dispel. He really loved mules and considered them superior to horses in every way. Bred only out of the very best mares, they were in fact very fine animals. I later stayed with him and met his wife and four of the loveliest children I have ever seen. Patty, aged fifteen, is particularly beautiful, both physically and spiritually, with that unselfconscious innocence which is totally ignorant of the censure of the world. They lived in a trailer house and one extra visitor tended to be a problem. Patty gave up her bed and slept with her younger brother. Like so many of the people I had met, the family had perfect natural manners, which bear no relation to the superficial veneer of knowing how to hold your spoon or how not to blow on your soup, but spring simply from a kind heart. Hesse used the expression 'little fart' as a term of endearment. This might not be appreciated by a society hostess, but I felt quite flattered! The family asked me to stay on for another day and go with them to the 'pole patch'. So early the next morning, accompanied by two cousins and with Jake the mule and one horse in tow, we drove into the mountains. The men cut down timber for posts and the animals hauled the cleaned tree trunks to the road, where they were cut into suitable lengths before being loaded on to the pick-up. Everyone pitched in. Meals were cooked over an open fire, a good day's work was done and we all had tremendous fun. I was particularly happy with Hesse and Linda, and when they left next day for the pole patch and it was time to say good-bye, I was very close to tears.

Once, riding through the mountains, I happened upon a sheep herder. I was dying for a cigarette, but had run out of matches. In the distance I saw a spiral of smoke and, having drawn the obvious conclusion that where there was smoke there must also be a fire, and that where there was a fire I could get my cigarette lit, I headed straight for it. Presently I came to a solitary caravan. A dear old man offered me a cup of coffee 'to go with my cigarette'. We smoked

and drank and chatted. The air was full of the scent of
baking bread. He asked me to stay and I said that I would
love to, provided there was suitable accommodation for the
horse. (The thought of suitable accommodation for myself
never even entered my head). There were two lovely large
grassy corrals, good hay, plenty of oats and the company of
other horses. Lara was literally in clover. I turned her out
and made myself at home. Presently, we took the dogs and
horses and went to look at the sheep. They were dotted
over the hillsides like so many fleecy clouds and only the
occasional tinkle of a bell broke the sun-drenched silence.
The dogs panted in the shade. We lay on the warm grass,
lazily watching the sheep and it seemed to me that the whole
scene had a strangely biblical quality. I asked Henry whether
he didn't get bored, living completely alone for months on
end. No, he said, every day he learned something new
about the sheep and the mountains. I asked what he did all
day, apart from checking the sheep night and morning. He
fished, he hunted, he sat and dreamed. I had noticed that
there was not a single book, or even a magazine, in the
caravan, and asked why. He had no desire, he said, to read.
Neither did he want a radio or any other form of communication with the outside world. Many professional men
disillusioned with the sterility of city life, became sheep
herders. He told me that coyotes caused a lot of damage and
that one might destroy as many as thirty sheep for the sheer
pleasure of killing; that once a flock had been attacked by
bear, it was a long time before it would again allow a
black sheep in its midst; a good herder soon learned to
recognise each individual sheep. . . . There was no hurry,
nowhere to go, and we sat on, talking. Later, Henry went
to the creek and returned in less than ten minutes with
eight lovely trout—but for me this virtuoso performance

was marred by the fact that he cut them open while they were still alive. The caravan was small, but Henry was a man of method and kept it very tidy. A thermos of coffee was always on hand, ready for immediate use; cigarette smoke spiralled pleasantly through the air and no one bothered to empty ashtrays or to open windows. And in this congenial atmosphere we sat and continued to enjoy one another's company. I used Henry's bed and he pulled out another for himself. The bed clothes were none too clean; but no matter—I was none too clean myself and slept well anyway. At five o'clock next morning, after making a fresh thermos of coffee, Henry went to look at the sheep and I slept on. All sheep herders are reputed to be excellent cooks, and mine was no exception. Breakfast was a Lucullan feast and I did it full justice. Six trout, two eggs, freshly baked 'biscuits', butter, jam and coffee did I consume, and dear Henry took this display of gastronomic voracity completely for granted and seemed so happy to feed me. When I left, he kissed me good-bye. I don't know why this experience should have made such an impression on me: perhaps it was the cameo-like quality of the encounter; perhaps it was a question of communication; but it was one of the nicest things that happened to me in America.

There was a sad sequel to my meeting with Henry. By the purest chance I happened some days later to stay with a Mrs. Powell, who turned out to be Henry's employer. She told me that two other sheep herders worked for her, both 'wetbacks', a term applied to Mexicans, who used illegally to enter America to find work by swimming the Rio Grande. The next day, at Soda Springs, the sheriff kindly agreed to put up the horse. He told me that he had just returned from Jackson hospital, where a young Mexican sheep herder was lying gravely ill, after being shot through the head by a colleague. Now he had to go and interview their employer, Mrs. Powell, who lived not far away. To my great relief, Henry was not involved, but the sequence of events struck me as very coincidental.

I heard a lot about the crime rate in America, with particular reference to robbery and to rape. I suppose that I was lucky, but at no time was my purse or person tampered with. Sometimes I carried large amounts of money, especially after cashing a $500 traveller's cheque; and I was constantly being advised 'to hide it very carefully'. The most ingenious places were suggested: but none, to say the least, was practical, and it seemed very much simpler to carry it in my pocket. When I came to America, it never occurred to me to be afraid. But gradually, as everyone warned me to be careful, I did begin to worry—I was literally brainwashed into it—but fortunately nothing untoward occurred. Personally, I never saw any violence; but I did hear one particularly bestial story. At Hallowe'en the children go from house to house collecting sweets and chocolate. Some people, apparently, cut open the sweets, insert a broken razor blade, carefully wrap them up again, and give them to the children. And such cases are not uncommon.

I was forever being advised to ride through the mountains, rather than to stick to the roads, and once, very much against my better judgment, I did so. From Victor to Swan Valley, via Rainey Creek, is a distance of some twenty-five miles. The trail, I was assured, was good and so long as I stuck to the creek it would eventually bring me out into the valley. However no sooner did we turn off the gravel road on to the horse trail, than our troubles started and almost immediately we lost the track. This would have been the moment to turn round and go straight back, but I felt ashamed to give up so easily and decided instead to enter the creek and ride along it until I could pick up the trail further on. Lara did her best, but there was no easy way down. We floundered around on the bank, getting caught up in logs and creeper infested undergrowth and were soon drenched from head to foot. After a really bad five minutes, we found the track, but now I was committed to go on, as nothing on earth would have induced me to retrace my steps: as it was, Lara had nearly broken a leg. For the next few miles, all went well. The trail crossed and re-crossed the creek and Lara followed it like a veteran. At one point we passed three men fishing, but were otherwise completely alone. The solitude was frightening. The place was full of bear, the trail almost non-existent. Presently we came to a complete standstill. Sheer granite mountains hemmed us in and there was no apparent way forward. I tried to lead Lara through the creek, but it was full of vast, slimy boulders and she slipped and plunged around. She tried to climb the bank, but lost her footing and came down—it was an absolute nightmare. There was no choice but to go back. We lost the trail again and I began to panic. I shouted, but the silence was absolute. So I followed the creek back up and eventually, weak with relief, came back to my three fishermen. Luckily they were going home in an hour, so I unsaddled Lara and let her graze. Considering the terrible damage there might have been, things were not too bad. She had a nasty deep, wide gash, almost to the bone, behind and just under her near fore knee; but it was only bleeding a little and didn't appear to bother her. I sprayed it with disinfectant and when the men came back, we started home. It was not much further to Swan Valley, but the greater part of the trail had been washed away and I could never have got out on my own. We had to lead her, as the path was often dangerously narrow, or else a solid mass of rocks and boulders. Once a fallen tree blocked the way. Lara hesitated to jump from a standstill and we led her past it through the creek. She behaved perfectly, but it still needed the four of us to test the depth of the water, the strength of the current and the soundness of the banks. I was desperately grateful for their help. If it hadn't been a Saturday, they wouldn't have been there at all and then goodness only knows what would have happened. When we reached the road we said good-bye and I led Lara to the nearest suitable place, about two miles down the road. As it turned out, luck was still with me. This was owned by Avery Weeks, a very influential man in the valley, and he and his wife looked after us for the next four days, going to endless trouble and helping in every possible way until Lara was well enough to be ridden on. The vet refused to come, saying it was a bad place to stitch; we were just to give her three shots of combiotin—for some obscure reason he insisted they be given in the breast—to spray the wound with disinfectant and to leave her in till it was better. After standing in for one night, her leg looked like a balloon and she couldn't put any weight on it. I immediately turned her out and after four days the leg was down, although the wound still looked very nasty: but she was perfectly sound and I decided to ride on, taking it very quietly for the first week or so. Everyone advised me to try something different—a purple spray, some red oil, and finally a yellow spray, Furazone, which was by far the best; but better than all three put together was a dog, which licked Lara's wound very thoroughly one night and next morning it looked so clean and beautiful as to be almost unrecognisable. From then on, she never looked back and by the time she left the States her leg was virtually unblemished. This was the only accident we had throughout the trip, and the only time Lara was in any way sick or sorry. For anyone used to the mountains, the ride would have presented no difficulty: I was too inexperienced and should never have attempted it on my own.

Riding in Idaho and Utah, I stayed with a great many Mormon families. I realise, of course, that there must be a fair quota of bad Mormons, but it so happened that all those I met were exceptionally fine people. From everything I saw and heard, I found the Mormon religion very impressive: certainly it is eminently practical and sensible and surely any religion that can persuade its members voluntarily to part with one-tenth of their income must have something special to recommend it! To forego tea and coffee was no great hardship, but to go without cigarettes was a different kettle of fish altogether. I never smoked in a Mormon home or, for that matter, in any other home where nobody else smoked; but when things got too desperate, I would slip outside for a bit of deep inhalation—of smoke, needless to say, not air. The general atmosphere, however, was not conducive to smoking and had I stayed in Mormon territory a little longer, I might well have given up the disgusting habit altogether.

I stayed with people of many different religious denominations and sometimes they would pay me the compliment of asking me to go to church with them. Although some of the services struck me as being very theatrical, with an awful lot of moaning and alleluiahing, I always found them interesting and really tried to enter into the spirit of the thing. Once I was invited to join a 'family home evening'. The Mormon Church encourages its members to spend one evening together as a family. It really doesn't matter what they do, so long as they do it together. On this occasion, we listened to a tape, lasting one-and-a-half-hours, concerning various prophecies about the Jews in Israel. It was quite interesting, but the children must have been bored stiff; yet they all behaved perfectly and just quietly fell asleep when they were exhausted. I believe there is another sect which tests the faith of its members by taking rattlesnakes to church and letting them crawl all over them, but unfortunately I never came into contact with any of its devotees. I made a special point, at the very end of my holiday, of going to Pennsylvania to stay with the Amish people.

One of the nicest and, to me, most surprising things about America was the genuine depth of religious feeling I encountered there. For many people religion is still a very real part of daily life. Nobody was embarrassed to talk about it; on the contrary, they seemed delighted to have an opportunity of doing so. I was absolutely astonished when I first stayed in a home where grace was said: but I soon got the message and waited a while before picking up my knife and fork. The majority of families with which I stayed said grace. Sometimes it was said aloud, sometimes silently. Any member of the family might be called upon to 'ask the blessing', and this would range from the simple 'God is great, God is good, bless this food. Amen' of the very young child to the more mature reflections of the adult. Often people would thank God that I had come to their house and ask Him to bless me and my horse and to protect us for the rest of our journey. This never failed to touch and, cursed fool that I am, to embarrass me. Sometimes I was asked if I would like to say grace, but could never bring myself to do so. On ranches it was a common sight to see twelve or fifteen grown men, seated round a single table, bow their heads and fold their hands in prayer, and I found this strangely moving.

In Wyoming I had met two delightful families, both members of the Mormon Church, who were there on holiday. They lived near Salt Lake City in Utah and I had promised to look them up, if and when I got that far. I now did so and soon Lara was installed with one family and I with the other.

I had vaguely planned to ride on through Southern Utah to Arizona and New Mexico. But this would have meant crossing a lot of desert with possible water and accommodation problems and it seemed childish to put Lara through all that just for the satisfaction of being able to say that we had done it. Finally, after lengthy discussions, it was decided that Lara could rest up for a week, while I went sightseeing. We could then ride on through the Colorado mountains, and from there truck to Lexington, Kentucky and continue on through the Virginias, so as to enjoy the much vaunted beauty of their Autumn foliage. This plan seemed sensible on all counts and particularly appealed to me as it would also give me the opportunity of seeing some of the Southern and Eastern states.

Each member of the Andersen family, with whom I stayed, was large—with a heart of gold to match. Lynnett, their daughter, drove me into town to arrange my sightseeing. To my horror, the cost of a three-day tour of Zion, Bryce and the Grand Canyons was $150. We went to lunch to discuss the situation, but finally decided that it would be silly not to go. Back at the tourist office, we were told that the first available vacancy was in two weeks' time. Lynett suggested taking sleeping bags and driving down together. At home, Fred and Emma, Lynnett's parents, wanted to come too. So finally we took the camper and set off en masse. At one point in Southern Utah we decided to take a small turn-off marked 'Vermilion Castle'; and the rock formations were so beautiful and the colours so vivid, that it would have been worth coming to America just to see this twenty mile detour. We admired Zion Canyon, its grandeur softened by the rays of the setting sun. We stopped at the Bumbleberry Motel and ate large slices of Bumbleberry pie. We looked over the North rim of the Grand Canyon, to which no picture can do justice, so frighteningly vast is it. To have ridden Lara down it, as I had rather naïvely planned, would have been completely out of the question as, apart from anything else, permission to do so would never have been granted. The horses and mules used for this purpose spend the first year or so carrying a pack and only then are they entrusted with a human cargo. We stopped to admire exotic gardens with paradise flowers, peach trees and humming birds. We saw Bryce Canyon, whose rock formations are marvellously delicate, with colours ranging from palest cream, through every shade of pink and scarlet, to richest ochre. All these canyons must also look entrancing by moonlight. But enough is enough. By now everything was beginning to blur and I could hardly be bothered to stop just to admire yet another scenic wonder. I was beginning to miss Lara and it was good to be home again.

Before leaving, I was shown round Salt Lake City. We looked at Temple Square, the Tabernacle and the organ, and listened to the famous Mormon choir. My main impression was a sense of wonder at the beauty and precision of work built long ago with loving care, albeit without the doubtful benefits of modern technology.

The Andersens were so kind. Concerned about the approaching cold weather, Emma not only insisted on giving me an anorak, which I am sure they could well have used themselves, but also on sewing slits into the sides, so as to make it more comfortable for riding! Throughout the trip, people were very generous with clothes. I had a favourite shirt and every time a new hole appeared, I would iron on a fresh patch, until eventually the thing began to look like a crazy quilt. Finally someone persuaded me to part with it and accept another in its place; and by the same painful process, I gradually acquired a new wardrobe and in the end only managed to hang on to my boots.

In the meantime, Dewaine had looked after Lara beautifully and the rest certainly did her good—but I know that she missed me. The next hundred miles or so were barren and deserted, so Dewaine and Evelyn, together with their dog, which gloried in the splendid name of Guppenheimer, very kindly drove us as far as Vernall. This was a full day's outing, yet, despite the time and expense involved, they refused to hear of any payment. At Vernall we stopped at the rodeo ground and after making sure there was absolutely nothing else they could do, they wished me luck and drove home. How can one ever repay such kindness?

Of all the states I rode through in the West, Utah has the greatest natural variety; and with its mountains, lakes, forests, deserts and canyons is, I think, far more interesting from a scenic point of view than either Wyoming or Colorado.

Two very pleasant changes occurred about this time: first, the mosquitoes disappeared; and second, the weather became much colder, thus obviating the necessity for getting up at the unearthly hour of four in the morning. Poor Lara didn't know what to make of the climate. It was still very hot during the day, but freezing at night. Obviously she decided that discretion was the better part of valour and, by the beginning of September, had grown her full winter coat. In the previous year Steamboat Springs, which now lay just ahead, had had a six foot fall of snow on the 1st September, and it was already the 26th August. I hoped the snow would hold off for a while, but realised that it would be prudent to have left the high mountains by, at the very latest, the middle of September. In fact we reached Denver on the 16th September without having run into any snow and left for Kentucky two days later.

Once, in the West, I nearly struck gold. I still had six pound notes and went into a bank to change them into dollars. The young cashier looked doubtful and went off to fetch a more experienced colleague. This lady didn't hesitate. First, she carefully looked up something in a book. Then she wet her fingers. I watched in fascination as she peeled off twenty dollar bills: fifty . . . one hundred . . . one hundred and fifty . . . and still she showed no sign of letting up. Finally I stopped her. Did she realise the exchange rate was roughly two-and-a-half dollars to the pound? Really? How very kind of me to point it out. Counting more slowly now, she gave me $14.60 and with this paltry sum I left the bank. I often wonder what she looked up in that book.

In Colorado I encountered my first language problem, when the man with whom I happened to be staying casually remarked that his cow 'had a hitch in her git-along'. That is to say, but more prosaically and with considerable less charm, that it was lame. This same man had a pet fawn which was hooked on television. If the set happened to be switched off, it would stand in front of it and imperiously stamp its little hoof until someone obligingly switched it on. Then it would settle down with evident contentment to hours of delicately wide-eyed, indiscriminate, viewing.

Most chance encounters proved to be great fun. Once, for a change, a lost motorist stopped to ask me for directions. I explained that I was a stranger and we continued on our separate ways. Ten minutes later, back came my motorist and informed me that we were stopping for a picnic. His two little girls would love to hold the horse while I ate and rested. This seemed a splendid idea and ever willing to oblige, I ate two hot dogs, grapes, chocolates, doughnuts, a banana and root beer. My new friend told me that he was an oil man from Texas on his way to a conference of missionaries at Salt Lake City. When I had eaten, he took three photographs, of which he gave me two, said good-bye and drove off—this time, unfortunately, for good.

Another time a group of picnickers called to me to stop and help them eat some freshly-caught trout. A rest wouldn't do Lara any harm, I thought, so I tied her to a tree in the shade and joined them. There were three families, all wonderful people. In addition to bringing up their own children and leading very busy lives, they had for the past twenty years also found the time to foster other peoples' children, often so severely handicapped as to be virtually moronic. They had a little deaf and blind girl with them and looked after her with the greatest tenderness and love. My admiration for such people, who actually do something instead of just explaining why they can't, is unbounded.

Other encounters, however, were less amusing. I was riding along a fairly well used gravel road when suddenly, completely out of the blue, a fully grown stallion came thundering down from the hilltop. I shouted and tried to keep him away with my headcollar but he just rushed round snorting and making stallion noises and I had absolutely no idea what to do. After a while he galloped back to his mares and as I was afraid to ride on, I went back to a nearby ranch, where three men were watching the fun. By now the stallion was back again and I asked the men for help: but they just laughed and told me not to be stupid; this was the horse's pasture; I should just hit him over the head and ride on. I had no option and with my heart in my mouth, trotted off along the road as fast as ever I could, until eventually we lost him. Fortunately Lara wasn't in season, but what, I wonder, would have happened if she had been? I know there is a short answer: but in all seriousness, I do think such a situation which, apparently, is perfectly legal in Colorado, could result in a very nasty accident.

Hunting is immensely popular in the West. I doubt whether the basic driving force is to augment the family larder. More likely hunting proves something to men about their masculinity. I heard amazing stories of ineptitude and personally came across a lot of accidents. I stayed at one home where the older boy had an artificial leg. He told me that, out hunting, a single bullet had shattered his leg and then continued on into his brother's ankle. At another place a a young boy had killed his cousin. It was no uncommon occurrence to lose a horse out hunting. Even cows and sheep were not immune and one aspiring nimrod shot not one pig, but the entire litter. Of course the locals blamed these accidents on people coming in from the towns who 'shoot at anything that moves', and certainly one met a lot of sporting-looking gentlemen, primed with whisky and armed with automatic rifles. But everyone seemed to enjoy hunting, irrespective of their age and sex. Ten-year-olds with mournful-looking hounds would be out after 'coon. Dear old ladies, a cane in one hand, a gun in the other, would prowl the woods in search of squirrel. Suffice to say that once the various open seasons start, one's life can seriously be endangered and we were lucky to escape unharmed. The first time Lara heard a gunshot at close range, she had such a fright she lost her footing and came down; after a while she learned to take no notice.

Peoples' kindness far exceeded the bounds of hospitality. On my birthday, I happened to be staying with Corky Keen who trains racehorses at Fort Collins. By a strange co-incidence Mrs. Keen had had her birthday the day before and I happened to mention that it was mine that day. At dinner that evening I was handed a beautifully wrapped box and inside nestled a gold chain and pendant. These two people on whom I had never even set eyes until this morn-ing, knowing that I was in a strange country and all alone, had wanted to make sure that I received at least one present. Next day they drove me to Denver racecourse to await trans-port to Lexington and I spent my last night in Colorado in a tack room. Early next morning, having loaded up, I waved good-bye to the West and set off for Kentucky.

Here are some last random impressions of the West.

The pace of life is very relaxed and so are the people. Their kindness has to be seen to be believed. Things have changed very little: men still tote guns, chew tobacco and, if they are very polite, use spitoons.

The women seem particularly happy and contented; probably because out here men are still men and there is no nonsense about women's lib. They are excellent cooks—definitely not the supermarket variety—hence my somewhat unseemly preoccupation with food. But why is margarine always used and never butter? And why do so many women go round in curlers, even on the street?

The people are fantastically lucky and know it. Every-thing they could possibly want is right on their doorstep: hunting, fishing, shooting, skiing and the most beautiful countryside imaginable. They love the West as it is and possibly this helps to explain their deeply conservative outlook.

One is always conscious of the country's youth. Many of the towns are ugly and seem just to have been thrown to-gether any old how. Trailer houses, which are ubiquitous, add to the general air of impermanence. The Indian reservations also have living quarters, many of which seem temporary and by no means a permanent part of the landscape. By contrast, the barns are absolutely beautiful and of great architectural interest. Nearly every home has its quota of plastic flowers and fruit: what is wrong with fresh ones?

The medical facilities seem to leave a lot to be desired. I was repeatedly told that, no matter how seriously ill or wounded you were, no doctor would come to you; somehow or other you had to get to him. The educational standards, too, appear to be very low. One sixteen-year-old girl returned from registering for her classes and was only taking three academic subjects! And nobody appeared to think anything of it.

Directions are always given in terms of East, West, North and South. To me this was useless, as I can only understand right, left and straight on. Western horsemen have good seats and an excellent sense of balance, but for the most part lack finesse. They seemed to me to be very careless of their horses' welfare.

These impressions are entirely personal and subjective. They must inevitably appear somewhat lop-sided, since I spent all my time in the country and avoided big cities like the plague. However, I record them for what they are worth.

CHAPTER FOUR

The South and East

THE ONLY ADDRESS I knew in Lexington was Hayes Haven Farm, where I had briefly changed vans on the journey out and I therefore asked to be taken there. This is a typically beautiful Lexington farm, with post and rail fencing, sheltered paddocks and large airy boxes. Mr. and Mrs. Hayes, and in particular their son Billy, were very kind to me. I was shown how tobacco—the popular Burley tobacco of Kentucky—is grown and dried; I was taken on a tour of their veterinary hospital, specialising in orthopaedic cases, and having some of the most up-to-date equipment in the country; and we visited the Racehorse Training Centre, with its covered oval track, permitting year round use. When it was time to leave, Mr. Hayes refused to accept any money, merely remarking, with typical Southern graciousness, that it would be payment enough if I were to remember them.

The area immediately surrounding Lexington is probably unique and I now rode through the very heart of it, along the famous Paris Pike. There stretched before me mile upon mile of gleaming white fencing and behind every fence grazed horses, and still more horses, and every horse was unmistakably stamped with quality. The houses were large and beautiful; the lawns immaculate. Curving driveways led to pillared porches; and over all this, with its air of gracious permanence, ancient trees stood sentinel.

The Hayes had given me the name of friends with whom to stay and here again I experienced the full warmth of Southern hospitality. A luxuriously appointed guest house was put at my disposal, a barn and paddock at Lara's. When I turned her out, she galloped round, bucking and kicking like a two-year-old and I rejoiced in her well-being and joy of life.

I had never seen a Tennessee Walking horse and as there was a large and famous stud nearby, Mrs. Lee drove me over. The owner very kindly devoted considerable time to showing me round and to answering all my questions and and then—again the Southern turn of phrase—thanked Mrs. Lee 'for having afforded her the pleasure of my company'. The Tennessee Walking horse was originally used by the plantation owners for riding, as safely and comfortably as possible, around their estates. Now it is purely a show horse. The more brilliant and dramatic its action, the more successful it will be and much time and trouble, as well as gadgetry, is devoted to improving its natural characteristics. I was to see many more Tennessee Walking horses and always felt sorry for them. They reminded me of women with platform soles. At best, the way they are shod is unnatural and must surely be bad for their legs and joints; at worst, they are subjected to downright cruelty.

From Lexington I rode on through the Daniel Boone country. Now the houses were smaller and less opulent, but still redolent of the South. Their wooden structures were painted white, with gaily coloured shutters; and each house had its porch, and each porch had its swing, and each garden its little patch of lawn. And everywhere black Sambo statues, with arms outstretched and soulful-looking eyes, seemed mutely to reproach me as I passed. There were other, less pleasant reminders of the South, such as the virulence of the anti-black feeling I encountered. Presumably feelings were mixed, and I found it perplexing and indeed hard to comprehend some of the comments made to me, a passing stranger, to whom my hosts showed such kindness and willingness to help in every possible way. I listened because I wanted to understand. This attitude cut across all barriers of class and of age. I don't pretend to know how typical it was: only that it was sad and shocking.

Only once did I encounter a deliberate case of meanness. I stopped at a livery barn and asked if I could put the horse up for the night. The owner wasn't there but a young man, who appeared to be in charge, said that that would be all right. As the box was filthy and there was no straw, he agreed to let me use inferior hay for bedding. No sooner said than done and after making sure that she had plenty of good hay to eat and her usual feed of oats, I went to meet some friends. Just as I was leaving I ran into the owner, who said we were most welcome and that anything on the premises was entirely at our disposal. An hour later I was back and saw at once that all the good hay had been carefully removed and the rubbish off the floor put in its place. And since her manger was completely empty—and normally her feed would last all night—her oats had clearly gone the same way as the hay. I knew she wouldn't touch the bad hay and would therefore spend the night entirely without food, but didn't dare to make a scene. Next morning, with the utmost warmth, the owner said to go ahead and feed her. But almost immediately he sent me on some trifling errand and on my return the food had gone again. Poor Lara! There was obviously no point in hanging around and the owner wished us bon voyage and waved us on our way. However, it behoves us to be grateful for small mercies, and at least there was no charge!

Whilst in Kentucky I was invited by Morehead University to give a lecture on the trials and tribulations of long distance riding in the States. To my shame, I declined this signal honour, since to ride across America is one thing, to face a bunch of students quite another, and my courage just wasn't up to the latter. However, we did spend two very enjoyable days at the university, which has a large agricultural complex with excellent stabling facilities. Lara was much admired and I was able to enjoy the company of the students and to relax.

Another honour, albeit not so signal, was when we were asked to appear on television. Again, my natural inclination would have been to refuse, but Jimmy and Duel Terrango, with whom I was to stay, had gone to so much trouble that to do so was unfortunately impossible. Actually, the whole thing was rather funny. I was to be televised as I arrived, riding down a steep hill, crossing a narrow bridge, dismounting in front of the house, unsaddling the horse and disappearing with her into the stable. Duel was particularly anxious for her husband to appear on television and so he joined us coming down the hill. Then Lara and I were on our own. But it was difficult to look gay and insouciant as we crossed the bridge, since the reporter had driven her car over the edge and there it hung, precariously poised, leaving us only a dangerously narrow gap through which to squeeze. The next 'shot' was disrupted by the camera breaking down, and I mounted and dismounted in front of the house like a yoyo, until I began to feel like the proverbial puppet on a string. This bored Lara, who now acted like a prima donna, looking thoroughly fed up and refusing to prick her ears until, with a final swish of her tail, she flounced into the welcome obscurity of the stable. By the time we had rescued the car and the reporter had told us in great detail the life story of every horse she had ever known, there was no time left for an interview and she had to dash back to the studio to catch the late edition of the news. We all wondered what the announcer would find to say and certainly nobody felt sanguine about the result: but promptly at eleven, taut with first night nerves, we all sat huddled round the box. At least we appeared in good company. First came President Ford, then Emperor Hirohito, then Prince Sihanouk of Cambodia and then Lara. I was so excited that I never heard a single word of what was being said. But Lara looked quite beautiful and we were all thrilled to bits—especially dear Duel, who was positively ecstatic. Oddly enough, although that channel was shown in six states, I never met anyone who saw us and only when I returned to England did I come across a woman who remarked that she had seen me on American television.

Whilst I very much enjoyed the people of Kentucky, the actual riding was very dull. I had been directed to follow old route 60 virtually all the way across the state and felt there must have been a pleasanter way to go: but if there was—and I asked repeatedly—no one suggested it and it was something of a relief to cross the state line into West Virginia. Yet I did so with some trepidation. Again and again I had been told that the further East one went, the more unfriendly were the people, and that this was particularly true of those living in the Appalachian Mountains. My own feeling was that the basic difference lay between town people and country people, rather than between country people in one area and those in another, and this subsequently proved to be correct. However, if one is to generalise, the people in the East were slightly more suspicious and reserved and I noticed that the women hesitated to make decisions without first consulting with their menfolk. But once this initial barrier had been overcome, they were every bit as friendly and warmhearted as their Western counterparts. The so-called hillbillies—and in the mountains this is strictly a term of approbation—were especial fun. Their speech was often hilarious, so down-to-earth and pithy was it, and for the first time I regretted not having a tape recorder. So many examples spring to mind; but unfortunately none which any editor would care to print!

By contrast with Kentucky, the riding in West Virginia was magnificent. We crossed the Appalachian Mountains and everywhere, in joyous profusion, oak, cherry, maple, beech and walnut, interspersed with dark green pine, painted the slopes with flaming red and purple, with every shade of gold and brown and russet; and when the sunlight filtered through the branches, each leaf became an incandescent jewel, alight with softly glowing brilliance.

The Watoga State Park was particularly lovely and since it had cabins and other tourist facilities, I stopped at the main office and asked the superintendent whether there was anywhere a horse could stay. Although the stables were officially closed, he kindly opened them and said to make ourselves at home. The barn had roomy boxes with hay and straw and even a few oats. Better still, there was an all-electric kitchen with pots and pans and cutlery and opposite a bedroom and a bathroom. True, the barn lacked running water, but an outside tap still worked and the superintendent brought me blankets and a pillow. Nearby was a paddock, safely fenced with post and rails. It was like a miracle. In the middle of deep forest I had found a perfect little home with all mod. cons. There was only one problem. I had no food. But even here, Garden of Eden-wise, did God provide—although not very adequately. All around were apple trees and I soon found that if I sat down underneath a tree and waited, sooner or later an apple would drop into my lap. Unfortunately the deer were also partial to this bounty and in the dusk and early dawn, like silent shadows, they came and ate up all the windfalls. That evening three old ladies happened by. I enquired did they rent a cabin, as I should like to buy some food; but they had only come to see the deer. We talked a while and after giving me some sweets, appropriately enough called 'life-savers', and warning me to bolt the barn most carefully, they left. At nine o'clock, when everything was dark and I had gone to bed, a car horn hooted. I couldn't find the lights, but one of the old ladies shone a flashlight underneath the door. Visions of *Arsenic and Old Lace* flashed through my mind, but I went ahead and opened up the barn. Out of the goodness of their hearts my three old ladies had driven home and brought a jar of coffee, two bananas, a jar of gherkins, a wedge of home-made cake, a jar of peaches, a can of tuna fish, a loaf of sliced bread, some jam and two small tins of sausages and beans. They had also thought to bring a plastic plate, knife, fork and spoon; a cooking pot, two glasses and a tin opener! After a welcome meal I again repaired to bed, but at four-thirty was woken up once more by Lara blowing and snorting and rushing round her box. This time, as I padded through the darkness, I fully expected to bump into a bear, but despite her obvious terror there was nothing in the barn and I could only think there must be deer outside. Early the next morning we went out for a ride. Lara was like a two-year-old. She pranced around in great excitement, peering behind every tree and thoroughly enjoyed herself, until I began to wonder whether I wouldn't lose her altogether. It was so beautiful that I decided to stay on and that evening my three good fairies reappeared, this time with hot chicken and potatoes, cooked tomatoes, salad, cake and biscuits. One other car came by and as the driver was on his way to town, I asked if he would bring me back a book—any book would do. At once he handed me a paperback 'to which I was most welcome'; and next day was back with two more books 'to keep me going on the way'. How can such kindness be explained unless, perhaps, the forest really was enchanted?

West Virginia has a lot of strip mines and in these areas accommodation was often hard to find. Once as I was wondering where to stay, a car pulled up, the driver introduced himself as 'Shorty' Shultz, and said he would be glad to put me up. He looked a bit disreputable to say the least, but proved in fact to be an angel in disguise. He and his wife, Ann, were expecting guests to dinner: but despite the fact that these were due in less than half-an-hour, Ann's hair was still in curlers, Shorty had made no attempt to change and I saw no apparent sign of cullinary activity. But nobody seemed to care and as it wasn't my party, I relaxed and sat back to await developments. The guests duly arrived and presently we sat down to a dinner so soigné and served so beautifully, that no words of mine can do it justice. The pudding was a gastronomic fairy tale. A sparkling dish of silver; a gleaming lake of chocolate; every surface a rich mirror of reflected candlelight. And on this lake were delicate swans of pastry, with slender curving necks and whitest whipped cream plumage. But Ann's head was still adorned with curlers and nobody seemed aware of even the slightest incongruity. Before going to bed, Ann handed me a torch in case I had to find the bathroom. This was fortunate, as when I crept downstairs, a truly enormous rat was sitting on the lavatory. In the face of dire necessity I bravely stood my ground and happily the rat vacated the disputed seat of honour.

Whilst on this delicate subject, I once approached a strange front door and rang the bell. No sooner did the owner open it, than I told him I had two requests: one, could he hold my horse, and two, could I please use his lavatory. He seemed vastly amused and was only too happy to oblige. Another time, however, in much the same unfortunate situation, I was confronted by a cross-looking old biddy who, to add to all my troubles, was singularly hard of hearing. I made known my needs in ringing tones and in reply received a look of deep suspicion. Finally she asked where I had come from. Obviously this was going to be a lengthy business, so I apologised for having troubled her and hastily rode on. And at the next house I had better luck. Such are the vicissitudes of travel!

The old folk in the mountains seemed blithely to ignore their years. One splendid specimen with whom I stayed was over ninety if he was a day. The horse was in his barn and I assumed, since he had asked me home, that I was also being invited for the night. But as the shadows lengthened, he became progressively more nervous, until finally he said I couldn't stay. Since there were two bedrooms, I couldn't see the problem and asked why on earth not? It wouldn't be proper, he explained; adding that he had his reputation to consider and he wouldn't want his girl friend to get wind of it!

Having no wish to compromise his virtue, I gladly followed him to a small house nearby. There an equally old lady made me welcome and looked after me as lovingly as a mother. A commode was popped under my bed, lest I catch cold during the night; woolly bedsocks were provided to make sure my feet were warm; and by the same token a virginal flannel nightie, the first of my entire trip. And when I was tucked up for the night, she brought me chocolate cake and cream. I felt ashamed to let her wait on me but knew that, mother-like, such was her pleasure. I sat and watched her quilting and every minute stitch was absolutely perfect. Her eyes were bright and clear and she worked for hours without apparent strain. When I left she said that she would pray for me and worry every day until she knew that I was safely home again. And I knew her words came from the heart. So many people, young and old, had said the same and who knows but their prayers had helped to keep me safe?

Not everyone was blessed with perfect sight and two old people with whom I stayed were blind. One, as happy as a lark, had brought up seven grandchildren without ever seeing a single one. The other ran a busy home and only asked that things be put back in their place. Whilst there, I tore my jeans and asked if she could let me have a patch. This she did and also cut it out and sewed it on and made a perfect job of it.

My last stop in West Virginia was something of an accident. I was riding along happily in one direction when a van pulled up and the driver, somewhat the worse for drink, insisted that I stay with friends living in quite the opposite direction. Rather than argue, I turned about and in due course confronted his astonished friends. Presented with a fait accompli, they had to make the best of it and as it turned out we grew so to enjoy each other's company that far from staying one night only, I was still there five days later! With Cathy and Marvin there was never a dull moment. No sooner had I come than four-year-old Billy took me by the hand and showed me round the farm. In the evening we went deer hunting. Dave, who is eleven, took the four-wheel drive up steep and narrow trails; Marvin stood in the back, holding a powerful flashlight; I bumped around behind him, clinging on with one hand, a loaded gun, the first that I had ever held, clutched in the other. Having pointed out the safety catch when he first handed me the gun, Marvin now treated the potentially explosive situation at his rear with nonchalance; and in appreciation of his good faith, I did my best to keep the barrel pointing skywards. Luck was with us and, despite bright moonlight, we spotted two fine bucks. I had the flashlight, Marvin the gun. The whole thing struck me as a bit unsporting, but at least the job was done with two clean shots and death was instantaneous. We gutted both deer on the moonlit mountainside and when they had been skinned, consigned them to the deep freeze.

My only other hunt, in Colorado, was equally successful. On that occasion we were after rattlesnake and I sallied forth with what looked like an elongated pair of fire tongs. We searched around amongst the rocks and eventually heard the dreaded rattle. Seasoned hunters all agree that this is one sound with which familiarity signally fails to breed contempt, and only when its source has been located can the danger safely be considered to be past. Since a rattlesnake can only strike with the uncoiled part of its body, about one-third of its entire length, so long as you keep your distance everything should be all right. I held the poor snake by the neck and one of the men cut off its head; but throughout the journey home, as if in silent protest, it continued to wriggle and to writhe. Once there, we skinned and sliced it and later it was fried in herbs and butter as an hors d'œuvre. In fact rattlesnakes make excellent eating, tasting somewhat akin to chicken, but should be nice and plump to stabilise the ratio of bones to meat. Squirrel also resembles chicken, but is very much more tender.

The day after the deer hunt, Cathy drove me into town. People in these small towns are far too busy taking things easy to have time to rush around and the atmosphere is consequently friendly and relaxed. We talked to everyone and everyone, from the mayor to the dustman, talked to us, and it was all great fun. Marvin was no exception. A lawyer by profession, he enjoyed his work; but not exclusively. He also loved his farm, his hobbies and his family, and I admired him for making sure that he had ample time for them.

I also tried my hand at sheep herding. Dave wasn't feeling well, so Marvin asked if I would help bring in the sheep. The thought of riding anything but Lara scared me stiff and when I set off on a little quarter horse, my mouth was dry with terror. I never really got the hang of neck reining, but my mount so obviously wanted to co-operate, that after a bit I loosened up and even started to enjoy myself. And since the sheep were equally co-operative, we soon had all three hundred in the barn. This was only the third quarter horse I had ridden and my experience is obviously very limited. But having said that, I found them infinitely more receptive than the average riding horse in England. They stopped and started at the lightest touch and were extremely quick and handy. On the other hand they seemed to me to be uncomfortable—rather like riding a pneumatic drill—and even their most ardent fans agreed that they would be unsuitable for a ride such as mine. Temperamentally, they appeared to be ideally suited to their work and also to their riders. A quarter horse derives its name from being able to run a quarter of a mile faster than any other horse—although some devotees of the thoroughbred will dispute this. It seemed to me that they could equally well have got their name from their hind quarters. One trainer with whom I stayed bred quarter horses for racing. These obviously had a large admixture of thoroughbred blood: but I have never seen a thoroughbred with the vast muscled-up quarters on his yearlings and even on the foals. The difference was both striking and impressive.

Here are some more impressions, gleaned along the way:

The bacon, so crisply delicious, that it crumbles in your mouth; the joy of old-fashioned apples, with blemished skins, but which explode with juice when you bite into them; the sensible custom of offering guests a flannel as well as towels; the terrible, non-stop, advertisements on TV; the astonishing uniformity of American handwriting; my first sight of an Aspen and the wonderful discovery that nature can bring poetry vividly to life; the conviction that accurate directions are as rare as gold dust—and that the more familiar a man is with his territory, the more surely he will get you lost; the fact that never once throughout my trip did I see any poverty; and finally, the realisation that the American nation is truly homogeneous; that every individual whom I met, no matter what his origin, be it English, Irish, Scottish, German, Dutch, Italian, Jewish or Chinese, was first and foremost an American; which, if one considers the relative youth, complexity and vastness of the USA, is a remarkable achievement.

Before leaving America, I very much wanted to spend some time among the Amish and therefore arranged to truck the horse to Lancaster, Pennsylvania. The only trouble was I didn't know a soul there, Amish or otherwise, and the friend who took me over complained that never before had he been asked to drive to an unknown destination! I suggested that we first get to Lancaster and then stop to make enquiries: somebody would surely help. And, in fact, the very first person to whom we spoke directed us to Amish friends.

The Amish live a very simple life. They shun modern inventions such as television, cars and radio—in fact anything powered by electricity—because they feel these lead to sin. The women, and even little girls, wear long dark dresses and their hair is drawn back under a prayer cap. Their faces are gentle and full of peace and their looks belie their years. During the week the men wear flat straw hats and dungarees; but on a Sunday, dressed all in black except for coloured shirts, they look extremely dashing. The Amish have their own schools and at fourteen the children leave to help at home. Horses and buggies are their only means of transport. The courting buggies are usually spick-and-span and there are roomier ones for married couples. The men are clean shaven until they marry; thereafter they always wear a beard. The houses are lit by gaslight and gas refrigerators are used. Milking machines are powered by diesel and so are windmills, used for pumping water, whenever there is insufficient wind. The everyday language of the Amish is Pennsylvania Dutch; their Bibles are printed in old Gothic and in English and their services are held in German. These take place at various homes in turn and not in Church. There is a period of silent prayer before and after every meal. In both the homes I visited the last meal of the day was served at four o'clock, presumably because there was still milking to be done and everyone retires early for the night. Life is lived according to the Bible, of which they try to read a little every day. Biblical names are popular and during my brief stay in Pennsylvania I met a Jonas, Jacob, Miriam, Mary, David and Ezekiel. Nobody is ever idle. The women make virtually all their clothes and the excellence of Amish cooking is proverbial. So, too, is the efficiency with which their farms are run and their business conducted generally.

I stayed with a young couple, Miriam and Melvin. Miriam's mother introduced her as 'the mistress of the house'. To me she looked more like a little girl and had the simple faith of one. When she spoke of God her eyes lit up and her whole being was filled with animation. When I confessed to doubts about the existence of heaven and hell, she was so upset that tears literally filled her eyes and she begged me to stay on with them. In the evening, we sat together in the gaslit room. The men were still out milking. The women sewed and quietly talked. The furniture was sparse and strictly functional. Presently Melvin came and he and Miriam sat side by side, like two young children, one reading the Bible, the other crocheting. The whole house was an island of dignity and peace and I felt an outcast washed up on its shores. Saddened by all that I had lost, I envied them a better way of life.

One heard amazing tales about the Amish. I had been told they used elaborate courting rituals which culminated, prior to marriage, in the two young people sharing a bed but being separated by a board; and was told that this was absolute nonsense. I wondered what the younger generation felt about the restrictions of the Amish life. Many, it seems, are seduced by the promise of the outside world: a few come back; the majority do not. The Mennonites, which I believe was the original sect, have reached a compromise: they use electricity and drink and smoke, but in moderation; and they drive cars, but only after all the chrome is painted black. I asked whether they didn't mind being stared at all day long by passing tourists; and they most emphatically said they did. But let it not be thought that upright living and good fun are mutually exclusive. The second family with which I stayed was quite hilarious and we laughed and joked the day away. These are personal impressions. I have set down, as well as I remember, what I saw and heard and felt. If the facts are not entirely accurate, I ask indulgence and apologise.

Journeys have a life all of their own and mine gave up the ghost in Pennsylvania. The date of death was 27th of

October. I had come to see the Amish and had seen them. There was no point in riding any further. My journey, lacking purpose, lost its impetus and all I wanted now was to be home again. Fortunately I had kept in touch with Mike and when he 'phoned to say that he was picking up the American team at Kennedy and would I like a lift, I was only too delighted to accept. We really motored on, but Mike was an outstanding driver and Lara never had a smoother ride. We passed the New York skyline with its myriad twinkling lights and presently drew up at our destination. A word of explanation may be useful here. I had previously made arrangements for the horse to stay at Oyster Bay, Long Island, with Mr. and Mrs. Plumb. I had never met the Plumbs, but Frank of Murty Bros., the firm arranging our flight home, had given me their name. They have a holding stable and keep horses in transit.

I should prefer to draw a veil over what happened next. I was embarrassed then and am embarrassed now. Lara was put in and Mike dashed off to Kennedy. There then ensued what I believe is known in literary circles as a pregnant pause. This was broken by Mrs. Plumb, who asked if I had any transport. I said no. Would I like to use their car? I said that I would rather not. Where was my luggage? I indicated the two saddle bags. I think Mrs. Plumb mentioned something about the motel being very expensive, but tactfully didn't press the point. Of course I should have called a taxi there and then and driven straight to the motel. Instead, I heard a voice, presumably my own, asking if I could spend the night up in the loft. Whereas this might just be acceptable in the West, it must have sounded awfully odd in Oyster Bay. I honestly think poor Mrs. Plumb didn't know whether to laugh or cry. In the end she said the hay was baled and wouldn't be very comfortable and took me to the house. My diary records the incident as follows: 'I had nowhere to go, so Plumbs took me in.' Which, I suppose, is factually correct, but only goes to show how easily facts can distort the truth.

My suitcases and passport had been forwarded to John Crighton in New York and next day I went to fetch them. John, a business friend of my husband's, kindly acted as my New York post box and generally helped in any way he could. When I telephoned to say that I was coming, I mentioned that sartorially I wasn't up to Madison Avenue standards. Personally, I didn't care. After all, only the richest people can afford to dress so shabbily. But I didn't want to embarrass John in case the doorman saw fit not to let me in. John was very busy, but he did ask me to dinner, which was kind at such short notice, and I filled in time by walking round New York. Sometimes, just momentarily, one is blessed with clarity of vision. I saw New York and hated it. I hated it for what it did to people. They didn't walk, they scurried. Mentally and physically. And if you tried to talk to them, presumably too scared to stop, they simply rushed straight past! And this was Madison and Fifth Avenue. What on earth would it be like in Harlem or the Bronx? The Crightons' flat was splendidly immaculate, the dinner excellent. John and his wife, Toni, were New Yorkers to their fingertips. They loved their city and would not change it for the world. But the most opulent graciousness can often hide the greatest poverty and on this subject we were poles apart. Men need the open sky and sun and earth to live and breathe and to preserve integrity. I know with absolute conviction this is so. By ten o'clock we all felt tired and John telephoned the Y.W.C.A. to make sure they had a bed. Clean, cheap and only too respectable, I thoroughly recommend it to other impoverished travellers.

At breakfast the next morning I met three middle-aged Yorkshire lassies. It transpired that we had travelled virtually the same route, except that they had gone by Greyhound bus. Yet their America bore no relation to my America. Their every impression, whether of people, food or scenery, was completely different from my own. Which only goes to show that there is no one reality, but that each man makes his own.

Later I went shopping, dispensing dollars with a fine abandon. Why, I wonder, does one never take foreign currency as seriously as one does one's own? I finished off by having a twenty dollar haircut and then, clutching my battered suitcases, took the Long Island railway home. Two things in New York I liked very much. First, the brownstones which, far from being ugly and decrepit as I had for some reason thought, were warm and elegantly beautiful; and second, a simply gorgeous poster of a great big friendly thumbprint with a smiling face and underneath, in capitals, the words 'Thumbody loves you'.

When the train pulled in at Oyster Bay, I asked the local taxi drivers, a very nice young couple, for advice on where to stay. They had a little wooden hut and there we sat reviewing the situation. I had to spend another five days in America; my purse contained exactly sixty dollars fifty; the only motel cost thirty dollars a night and obviously I couldn't ask the Plumbs to go on looking after me. First my new-found friends brought coffee and some cookies. I don't think I looked all that poor and certainly didn't look hungry: yet kindly people kept on feeding me. We then fetched and perused a local paper and eventually found a furnished flat for twenty-five dollars a week. This seemed very suitable and I would still be left with money to visit Lara and to buy food. But when I telephoned Mr. Plumb, he wouldn't hear of it: I was not to budge an inch; just sit tight on my suitcases and he would be round to fetch me straight away. I did as I was told and nothing could have pleased me more.

I hesitate to say too much about the Plumbs; good things are often best left undisturbed. I adored Charlie straight away—I say this in all seriousness—and he fed my passion with ice-cream and chocolate sauce. Some people drain off energy and joy and leave only a greyness of the soul; others, by their mere presence, fill you with excitement and vitality. Charlie was like that. And I liked Meem too, very much indeed. She belongs to that select and fortunate band of women who, even if they live to be a hundred, will continue to look elegant. She prefers horses to housework and is definitely not the bottling/pickling type. If the mood was on us, nobody thought twice about ordering dinner from a restaurant and popping round to fetch it, and in this congenial atmosphere my new-found resolutions about being a better housewife died a natural death. I hasten to add that whatever Meem did cook was excellent: she simply didn't make a fetish of the thing. The house was large and comfortable, not smart, and full of dogs and cats, antiques and books and photographs. Whatever the elusive quality that goes to make a perfect host, Meem and Charlie have it. I think it has to do with making people feel completely free and yet completely welcome. Certainly it is natural and and wholly unobtrusive. Meem was usually busy in the barn, so Charlie organised little expeditions. Once, with Meem, we drove to Pennsylvania where their son, the captain of the American three day event team, was taking part in some event. I rode Lara every day, just to stretch her legs, but otherwise relaxed and took life easy. Both Meem and Charlie seemed to think it very funny that I had crossed the States not knowing how to canter. Charlie offered to teach me, but at that late stage I preferred to leave well alone. I spent my last few dollars on taking Meem and Charlie out to dinner. Apart from anything else, this satisfied my sense of tidiness. But Charlie disagreed and insisted I take forty dollars— just in case. As it turned out, I didn't need the money and returned it from the airport; but I appreciated the kindness of the thought. Charlie and Meem were my last friends in America and I was fortunate indeed to end my holiday in their company.

CHAPTER FIVE

Last Impressions

For the first time I thought about my trip. Starting in Nebraska, I had ridden through Wyoming, Idaho, Utah, Colorado, Kentucky, West Virginia, Virginia and Pennsylvania. I had spent four and a half months in America and covered some two thousand miles. The whole trip had been an unqualified success. Had it been worth the trouble and expense? Yes, yes and yes again. Of course at times you wondered how on earth you could have got yourself mixed up in such a crazy venture; what on earth could have possessed you to abandon the safe warmth of home for tired loneliness and discomfort. At times the vastness of the States seemed huge beyond belief and impossible to cross. But these fears and doubts were momentary and the good parts of the trip a thousand times outweighed the bad. Isolated facts are sterile things and I was fortunate to see America at first hand. I heard its speech. I smelled its grass, its trees, its refuse. I saw its colours, the quality of its light. And above all, I met its people.

Why, I asked myself, should these people, the real ambassadors of America, have been so kind to me? Obviously certain factors helped. I was a woman, not too ugly, travelling on my own, and I came from England. There was community of interest: I mainly stayed with horsy people and Lara forged an immediate link between us. People could relate to what I was attempting: they may have thought me mad, but they admired my spirit. When I asked Charlie why, knowing absolutely nothing at all about me, he and Meem had given me the freedom of their home, he said that anyone who had done what I had 'had to be all right', and I suppose that others must have felt the same. I was actually doing what so many people would have loved to do. In the nicest possible way they envied me and would have given a lot to come along. It was not a question of any particular destination: the mere fact of going somewhere, anywhere, of being able to break away, was all that really mattered. And finally, I really think that people liked me. At least I hope they did—if only half as much as I liked them.

Throughout my journey, I was repeatedly asked the same four questions: Isn't it terribly expensive to fly a horse over? Wouldn't it have been more sensible to have bought or leased a horse over here and then sold it before going home? Aren't you afraid, travelling all alone? And finally, will you write a book when you get back?

To fly a horse to the States *is* very expensive—about two and a half thousand pounds. A further £500 was spent on trucking the horse from New York to Nebraska, from Colorado to West Virginia, and again from Pennsylvania to Long Island, New York. This left £500 for actual living expenses for myself and the horse, to include shoeing, veterinary expenses, cigarettes, presents, postage and sightseeing, which would have been totally inadequate but for the kindness and unbelievable hospitality extended wherever I went. In fact, on my return to New York I still had £100 left.

Yes, of course it would have been more sensible to have bought or leased a horse in America and then to have sold it before returning home, thereby saving nearly £3,000. I had naturally considered this possibility before setting out, but had never seriously entertained it. Lara was my horse. I knew and trusted her. We would go together or not at all. And never, at any time, did I have cause to regret my decision.

No, I wasn't afraid. The fact that I had never been to the States before and didn't know anyone there didn't worry me in the least. People would mutter about vast distances, bears, rattlesnakes, rape, razor gangs and rampant crime generally. I ignored them and adopted the simple expedient of refusing to consider any such possibility. Ostrich-like, maybe, but effective. People the world over, given a chance, want to be kind and friendly and I saw no reason to think they would be otherwise in America. On the contrary, the warmth of American hospitality is well known. I reasoned that, once I landed in New York, there would be only one way to go—forward—and any problems that arose could be dealt with as and when they cropped up. Another popular suggestion was that it would have been better to have travelled with a companion. I preferred to go alone for a variety of reasons. Two or more people travelling for so long in such close proximity might well end up getting on each other's nerves; one would always be waiting for the other; and one could hardly, without grossly abusing their hospitality, ask strangers to look after two or more people and a corresponding number of horses. Both ways of travelling have their advantages: the decision as to whether to travel alone or in company really depends on what you want from a holiday. In the latter case, travelling with a pack horse, one could be more or less independent; one could explore much finer countryside; there would be the fun of sleeping under the stars, cooking over an open fire, hunting and fishing. Probably ideal for lovers and newly-weds. Not belonging to either category, I chose the former for two main reasons, one aesthetic and the other practical. The choice of route is obviously circumscribed by the necessity of finding a suitable place for the horse to stay each night; but the idea of being sheltered by strangers, like a traveller in the days of yore, appealed to me. I was thus privileged to meet people from every walk of life, to share their homes, their conversation and their way of life, and so to get the 'feel' of the country. In my opinion, the ideal way of achieving this is to travel alone on horseback. To turn up with any form of mechanised transport would be to invite the perfectly justifiable response that the nearest motel is only twenty-five miles on down the road! Obviously, the scenic beauties of a country are important: but in the final analysis the people *are* the country. From a more practical point of view, I really had no choice, since I am strictly a town girl with all the limitations that this implies. I can't light fires without a fire lighter, shoot or skin animals or fight off intruders. All I can catch is colds and the thought of icy mountain streams and below freezing temperatures helped to temper my enthusiasm for the more romantic aspects of life in the wilds. My stupidity was embarrassing. Having been told that if I ever got lost, all I had to do was to follow a creek or river downstream and I would eventually find people, I asked, perfectly seriously, how, if the land was flat, could I be sure which way the stream was flowing? As if this wasn't enough, I have absolutely no sense of direction and although I did have a compass with me, was never absolutely sure that I would know what to do with it should the necessity of using it ever arise. Lara, too, is really a town horse. She won't tether, hobble or even stand tied reliably on her own. Stalwart cowboys advised me just to turn her loose at night; if there was adequate grazing and water, she wouldn't stray far. I preferred to ignore this suggestion. In any case, she couldn't have travelled as she did without adequate oats and hay. Unlike me, however, she has an excellent sense of direction.

And finally, to the last question: 'Will you write a book

when you get back?' the short and truthful answer—at the time—was 'No'.

In retrospect, what I took proved to be fairly sensible. As it turned out, I never used the plimsolls, the shorts, the vest, the spare reins, the compass or, for that matter, the lariat; but it was still probably wise to take them. The shoeing kit was left in Nebraska, but the claw hammer would have come in useful. A camera, which, like an absolute idiot, I didn't take for reasons of space and economy, warm gloves and some hoof preparation, necessary owing to the very high temperature, low humidity and rough going, would have been excellent substitutes.

Experienced long distance riders may wish to skip this paragraph. I write for other amateurs like myself, *attempting the same kind of ride*. My only excuse for doing so is that I've done it and it works. It doesn't matter if you don't ride well. If you can't canter, trot; if you can't trot, just walk. If you want to hurry, you might as well take a car in any case. The only proviso, so far as riding is concerned, is that you should sit well enough not to give your horse either a sore back or a sore mouth. Keep things as simple as you can. The less you have, the less there is to lose and break. This applies especially to your tack, which should be cleaned every day. Don't take the thing too seriously. Have fun. Don't plan in too much detail and don't make precise time-tables. These can be tyrannical and anyway it doesn't work. Your rate of progress must depend entirely on how you and your horse feel at any given time. Journeys have a way of taking you, and the unexpected detour or event often turns out to be most fun. Have a rough idea of what you want and then play it by ear. Above all, remember two important C's— consideration and common sense. Consideration for the horse, which *always* comes first, and common sense for both of you. You won't get far without them; with them, given a pinch of luck, everything should work out very well. C for courtesy is also worth remembering.

People talk an awful lot—much too much in fact—about good luck. Of course luck is important and of course it plays a part in any venture. We were very lucky in lots of ways. But it is all too easy to confuse bad luck with lack of common sense and nine times out of ten, when people moan about their 'rotten luck', the truth is that, if they had had sufficient common sense, their so-called 'rotten luck' would never have materialised. A little common sense is worth an awful lot of expert knowledge.

The success of any trip depends largely on your mount. Certain things are absolutely basic. *You* should like your horse, since you are going to rely heavily on its company. And your horse should like *you*. If it does, it will at least try to co-operate, and nothing is more unpleasant than constantly having to worry about what your horse is going or not going to do next. Personally, I wouldn't take any horse under the age of eight. Between ten and twelve is probably ideal. Bone troubles are all too easily come by and a long distance ride, even doing it the way I did, takes a lot out of a horse. I took Lara to Wales to get her fit in March and flew home in November. This means that she was ridden almost continuously for nine months and during that period probably averaged ten to twelve miles a day, often over rough and difficult going. I doubt if a young horse could cope with that. It goes without saying that any horse, no matter what its age, must be completely sound. A long distance ride will very soon winkle out any weakness. Your mount should be safe for what you want. If you plan to go into the mountains, which might well mean narrow, precipitous trails, don't take a horse that is liable to panic. If you have to ride through traffic, make sure the animal is traffic-proof. And so on. Obviously, nothing can be guaranteed one hundred per cent and one wouldn't wish it so; but here again, use your common sense. And finally, a long distance horse MUST walk really well and be a comfortable ride. Otherwise you are in for an unpleasant trip.

So far I have said very little about Lara as a horse and nothing I can say can do her justice. In my opinion, she is an almost ideal long distance horse. Apart from having more than her fair share of the above qualities, she has many others. These may not be strictly necessary, but are the icing on the long distance cake. She is full of life, but sensible. Once she got out of her corral and trotted off down the road. I wasn't there, but apparently the owner called her by her name and she turned round and came straight back to him. She is intelligent, alert and beautiful: everywhere she goes, people admire her. Whenever I was asked if I would be prepared to trade her, my stock reply was 'Not for Secretariat'—and I meant it. She really enjoys being ridden; in a sixty acre field she canters up to have her tack put on, and she enters into the spirit of the thing, which makes the trip a thousand times more enjoyable. She has an independent turn of mind yet never takes advantage and is one hundred per cent genuine. She is gentle and affectionate and an ideal companion. I used the word 'almost' ideal advisedly. For an ideal long distance horse, she is too finicky about her food and not sufficiently placid to retain condition well. But having said that, I very much doubt whether the ideal long distance horse exists and Lara is possibly as close as you will get.

I make no apology for my apparent obsession with the horse: she didn't ask to be dragged half way across America and throughout the trip her welfare was my primary concern.

When she was going well and obviously enjoying herself, I was happy; when she seemed depressed or tired, I was sad. We depended on each other and this interdependence brought us close.

By far the most important single factor affecting Lara's condition was whether or not she settled wherever we happened to be staying. Any place where she had the company of another animal was usually fine and on her travels she had at various times as neighbours donkeys, mules, pigs, goats, calves and sheep, not to mention a raccoon and some coyote pups. A large barn, where she had plenty of room to move about, was ideal; in a confined space, her legs tended to come up behind. She invariably became absolutely hysterical, breaking out and rushing around, if she was put in a place out of which she couldn't see, or was herself shut in with other animals loose around her. So long as they stood right by the door, she was fine; but the minute they moved even a few yards, she would start to get upset. In such a case, I always asked that another animal be put next to her, and she immediately quietened down. In the West, she often stayed in corrals. Sometimes she settled, sometimes she didn't, and it was often difficult to understand why. Any wild animals, especially coyotes, excited her terribly and it would take hours for her to calm down enough to eat. The mosquitoes, too, were often a great nuisance.

If the quality of the food was first rate, there would be absolutely no problem about her eating up. But if anything was not to her taste, she would either refuse to touch it altogether or just pick at it. The overall quality of hay in the West was very good—far better and cheaper than in the East—but a lot of alfalfa was fed and for a long time Lara refused to touch it. Oats were mostly fed whole. They were usually very poor—all husk and no kernel—and at first I could only persuade her to eat them by smothering them with liquid molasses. Eventually she got used to them, but never ate them with any real conviction. Sweetfeed, a mixture of oats, corn, pellets and molasses, with added vitamins, was very popular and Lara ate it well. But it was far more heating than plain oats and, by trial and error, I found that ten pounds a day was as much as her legs could stand. If I managed to get eight pounds of sweetfeed and eight pounds of oats down her a day, I was happy. The bulk of this had to be fed at night, since in the morning she was usually too anxious to be off to eat much.

I was always being told: 'Just leave her; she'll eat when she's hungry.' No doubt. But the proof of the pudding is in the eating and I spent many guilty hours searching through hay lofts for a better bale of hay and through cornbins for more palatable feed: and as soon as I found something she liked, she would always tuck right in. If necessary—and nobody ever seemed to resent this—I would get suitable hay from elsewhere. If there was no grain, I would do my utmost to get some. Unfortunately one could rarely buy it loose and often the smallest quantity available was a hundred pound bag. In that case, I gave Lara as much as she would eat and left the rest behind. It was unfortunately not possible to turn her out in the West, as all the fields were fenced with barbed wire. In the East, wooden fences were quite usual and things were easier.

We averaged twenty miles a day in the West; rather less in the East. Our shortest ride was two miles; our longest thirty. Once we rode from Steamboat Springs, lying at 6,500 ft. over Buffalo Pass at 10,300 ft., and down again to about 6,000 ft. This was a ride of some twenty-five miles over fairly rough going and she made absolutely nothing of it.

Having come up gradually from Nebraska, we never had the slightest problem with the altitude. A lot of our riding was done at over 7,000 ft. and we several times crossed the Continental Divide.

We rode mainly at a walk. If the going was bad, she averaged four miles per hour; if good, five miles per hour, and when the mosquitoes were out, six miles per hour. Whenever the terrain permitted, and this was not often, we trotted on. Throughout the trip we never cantered, as I can't control her at that pace. About one-third of the time we were on tarmac. In fact this wasn't nearly as bad as it sounds, since many of these roads were narrow, almost traffic-free and really very pretty. Otherwise we used dirt and mountain roads. In Nebraska and West Virginia, the so called 'County' roads were of sand and very fine gravel and a pleasure to ride on; elsewhere they were covered with stones and grit of varying size and were very hard indeed on a horse's feet. Many of the larger roads had grass verges, known as bar-pits. These were very often wide, since they were originally built for herding sheep and cattle: but so far as horses were concerned, they were of little use, invariably being strewn with empty coke cans, broken bottles, barbed wire and every other kind of rubbish.

A day's ride would basically follow the same pattern. I would ride for an hour or so, then dismount and lead for a while. If I was saddlesore—which fortunately happened only once, oddly enough in the middle of the trip—this procedure was reversed. About half way, as soon as I came to a decent bit of grass, I would unsaddle her, put on her headcollar (which was carried tied to the saddle) and let her graze. If at all possible she would always have a roll. Usually we stopped for an hour or so, but if the grass was particularly good and we were not pressed for time, this might be stretched to two hours or even longer. Whenever we came to a creek or river, I always stood her in it while I had a cigarette and relaxed. This did her legs and my nerves a world of good.

Water was never any problem. There were always plenty of streams and I let her drink as often and, generally speaking, as much as she wanted. The only 'emergency' food I carried was buffalo jerky and apricot leather. Jerky consists of strips of dried salted meat, is very good and nourishing, and ideal for carrying around in saddle bags. Apricot leather is exactly what it sounds like—a leather-like substance made from Apricots—also very good. I took this stuff along purely in a spirit of fun, since there was never any question of necessity. In fact people often gave me sandwiches to take along; if I happened to be passing through a town, I could stop and buy a hamburger; and there were always fruit trees along the way. Once, by mistake, I bit into a walnut instead of an apple: the taste was vile beyond belief.

On these rides, I encouraged Lara to think for herself. If she wanted a drink, I let her make her own way to water; if she felt tired going up a hill, I let her stop until she felt ready to go on; if the going was rough, I let her pick her own way. Often, when she obviously considered she had gone far enough, she would slow down and look wistfully up and down suitable-looking driveways. In fact, she did everything but talk and we understood each other perfectly. In West Virginia, she developed an apple problem. It was a marvellous year for apples and there were laden trees everywhere you went. I would stuff my pockets and eat as I rode along. But as soon as Lara heard the sound of munching, her stride would shorten, her head swing round and only when she had had the core could we proceed. Actually, she must have eaten bushels of apples. At first I worried about how many she was having, but they never did her any harm and I soon stopped bothering.

The main roads often had a stony shoulder and this sometimes caused problems. Once one of the sheriff's men drove up to say that he had received a complaint that a horse was obstructing the highway. Was it me? I said that I supposed it must be, but pointed out that a car could always change its tyres, whereas a horse was stuck with one set of legs for life and I had to protect them as best I could. He just grinned and drove off.

On the whole, I found American motorists courteous and sensible. On straight roads I rode facing oncoming traffic, as cars tended to give us a wider berth that way; on roads with very sharp bends, I rode with the traffic. Whilst in England it is correct to ride on the left, in America no one seemed quite sure of the exact legal position. Contrary to what I had been told, nobody tried to run me down or otherwise to injure me and my worst complaint was that people would do an awful lot of hooting to ensure that I waved back to them! Even in the heaviest traffic, Lara was perfect.

Whilst on the subject of motorists, I was warned never, on any account, to hitchhike in America. Once, however, Lara badly needed oats and I decided to try my luck. A car stopped almost immediately. Three delightful students took me ten miles out of their way to collect the oats, waited until I was ready and then drove me all the way back again. And only after stopping to admire the horse and making sure that there was nothing else they could do, did they resume their interrupted journey. So much for never hitchhiking in America—although I do realise that one swallow doesn't make a Summer.

One final thought about long distance riding. I think my trip was a success for several reasons: but primarily not because of what I saw or who I met: but because it was completed on one and the same horse; because that horse, with one exception, was never lame or sick or sorry; and and because, after two thousand miles of difficult terrain, she looked glossy, sleek and well; better, in fact, than when she started. And this, in my opinion, is the real achievement of any long distance ride.

Our flight home had been booked for Tuesday, the 5th November, on the express understanding that a competent horseman with adequate veterinary knowledge would be on board. This was vitally important as Lara and I were flying on our own and I know absolutely nothing about injections and even less about coping with emergencies in mid-air. In the final analysis, a pilot has authority to shoot a horse, but this was something I was hoping to avoid. Since take-off time was five-thirty in the morning, a van was to collect us from the Plumbs at midday on the 4th and we would spend the night at the airport quarantine centre. Twelve o'clock came, two o'clock came, four o'clock came, but no van came. I telephoned Murty Bros. They were sorry. The horses they had been expecting hadn't come and consequently there was no attendant going back. If I wished to fly alone, they could still get me on tomorrow's flight. The next flight with an attendant would be either on the Friday or the following Sunday. They promised to let me know. It was all very embarrassing. I didn't dare to risk flying alone, yet hated to abuse the kindness of my hosts. Charlie was extra sweet. First he took my stuff back to the house and then he bought me an extra large ice cream— and I loved him for the thought. Next day, not having heard from Murtys, I telephoned to see if there was any news. All incoming flights were cancelled for an indefinite period, due to strangles. No flights coming in meant no attendants going out. Which left me three alternatives: I could postpone my flight indefinitely; I could pay the return fare and accommodation for an attendant; or I could fly alone. Really, it was a case of Hobson's choice and I arranged to fly on Friday, the 8th November. A van would collect us at twelve o'clock on Thursday. At three o'clock on that day a van from Murty Bros. did, in fact, arrive, but only to deliver horses. At four o'clock the telephone rang. Our van had broken down, but was now on its way. And finally, at 4.30, contrary to every expectation, we were off! At the airport, the driver found that he had only half of Lara's papers. He telephoned Murty Bros., who said that they would bring the rest. I decided not to give Lara any tranquilliser as I wasn't sure of her reaction, but seriously thought of taking one myself. But I did give her as large a feed of nuts as she would eat, because the only hay available was absolutely dreadful. It really worried me that her hay-net, the only 'distraction' on the flight, would not be one at all, and so it proved; for after spitting out one mouthful, she steadfastly ignored it throughout the eight-hour flight. We bandaged her and at five o'clock drove the short distance to the aeroplane. She went in like an angel, but the stall, instead of being open as it had been on the journey out, was enclosed by a canvas top, which kept on flopping round her ears—something I knew that she would hate. So far, so bad. A syringe was thrust into my hand with emergency instructions and we were on our own. Before take-off, the captain asked whether I had been shown how to use the oxygen equipment. I said I didn't think the horse would panic. He replied he didn't give a —— about the horse. Did *I* know how to use it? I hadn't meant to be facetious: it was just that in my mind the horse quite naturally came first. During take-off I stayed with Lara and she seemed quite calm. But when I tried to leave her, she started being silly, kicking and pawing and uttering frantic whinnies. The first officer came rushing out and I persuaded him to baby-sit while I went up front for a cup of coffee. For a while, Lara seemed to suffer from lack of air pressure: she constantly shook her head and yawned and yawned. But after an hour or so she settled down and I was free to come and go as I pleased. The crew was absolutely charming. They evinced great interest in my trip although, I suppose, my mode of travel must have seemed awfully slow to them. I was given a set of headphones and listened in to all the technical, and quite a lot of not-so-technical, chit-chat. There was a warning of turbulence ahead. The men strapped themselves in: but when I asked what about me, they only grinned and shrugged their shoulders. I also gathered that we were going to Prestwick—a fact that Murty Bros. had omitted to mention—to deliver, of all things, whisky and barbed wire. This being so, I asked the captain to arrange for hay and water, which he very kindly did. We only stopped a while— just long enough to offload Lara, then the cargo and then to load poor Lara up again; but now at least she had some hay to play with. As darkness fell, I made one last discovery. The flightdeck of an aeroplane, with all the instruments lit up, is surely the cosiest place twixt heaven and earth— especially when it contains a handsome crew. Although, I must admit, their cooking wasn't quite up to their looks. But even burnt food helps to make a journey memorable and altogether it had been a lovely flight. And now the lights of Heathrow multiplied below us. We dipped our wings in salutation, made a perfect landing and taxied to a stop. Lara and I were safely home again.